Vocabulary Games and Activities for Teachers

Peter Watcyn-Jones

Illustrated by Nigel Andrews

*To the coffee bars in Swansea and Malmö –
a constant source of inspiration and caffeine-poisoning.*

PENGUIN
ENGLISH

PENGUIN ENGLISH

Published by the Penguin Group
Penguin Books Ltd, 27 Wrights Lane, London W8 5TZ, England
Penguin Books USA Inc., 375 Hudson Street, New York, New York 10014, USA
Penguin Books Australia Ltd, Ringwood, Victoria, Australia
Penguin Books Canada Ltd, 10 Alcorn Avenue, Toronto, Ontario, Canada M4V 3B2
Penguin Books (NZ) Ltd, 182–190 Wairau Road, Auckland 10, New Zealand

Penguin Books Ltd, Registered Offices: Harmondsworth, Middlesex, England

Published by Penguin Books 1993
10 9 8 7 6 5 4 3 2

Every effort has been made to trace copyright holders in every case. The publishers would
be interested to hear from any not acknowledged here

Printed in England by William Clowes Limited, Beccles and London
Set in New Century Schoolbook

Contents

Introduction   v

Part 1 Teacher's notes   1
Part 2 Material for photocopying 23

Activity	Level*	Page
Ice-breaker activities		
1 Find someone who…1	I	24
2 Find someone who…2	E	28
3 Find someone who…3	I/A	29
Activities for dividing a class into pairs/groups		
4 Broken sentences 1	E	30
5 Broken sentences 2	I	31
6 Broken proverbs	A	32
7 Broken sentences 3	I	33
8 Word sets 1	I/A	34
9 Word sets 2	A	34
Bingo activities		
10 Picture bingo		
(teacher's board)	E	35
(students' cards)	E	38
11 Opposites bingo		
(teacher's board)	E	35
(students' cards)	E	39
12 Prepositions bingo		
(teacher's board)	I	36
(students' cards)	I	40
13 Synonyms bingo		
(teacher's board)	I	36
(students' cards)	I	41
14 Definitions bingo		
(teacher's board)	A	37
(students' cards)	A	42
15 Parts of the body idioms bingo		
(teacher's board)	A	37
(students' cards)	A	43
Matching pairs activities		
16 Verb + noun collocations	E	44
17 Mini dialogues	E	46
18 Who uses what?	I	48
19 Definitions	I	50
20 Collective/partitive nouns	I/A	52
21 Idioms	A	54
22 Funny definitions	A	56

Activity	Level*	Page
Domino-type activities		
Board for dominoes		58
23 Dominoes: Nouns 1	E	59
24 Dominoes: Nouns 2	I/A	59
25 Dominoes: Nouns 3	A	60
26 Dominoes: Clothes	E	60
27 Dominoes: Phrasal verbs	I	61
28 Dominoes: Idioms	A	61
29 Word association dominoes 1	E	62
30 Word association dominoes 2	I	63
31 Word association dominoes 3	A	64
Crosswords and word square activities		
Half a crossword activities		
32 Half a crossword: Sports, hobbies and pastimes	E	65
33 Half a crossword: Jobs and occupations	E	67
34 Half a crossword: Nouns	I	69
35 Half a crossword: Verbs	I/A	71
36 Half a crossword: Adjectives to describe people	I	73
37 Half a crossword: Types of people	A	75
Sort out the clues activity		
38 Sort out the clues	I	77
Word battleships activities		
39 Word battleships 1	E	79
40 Word battleships 2	I	81
41 Word battleships 3	A	83
Word grouping activities		
42 Word groups 1: Nouns	E	85
43 Word groups 2: Nouns	I	86
44 Word groups 3: Adjectives	I/A	87
45 Word groups 4: Verbs	A	88
46 Word groups 5: Idioms, etc.	A	89

* E: elementary   I: intermediate   A: advanced   All

Contents

Activity	Level*	Page

Pair work cards and board games

Pair work cards

Activity	Level*	Page
47 Definitions cards 1: Nouns	A	90
48 Definitions cards 2: Verbs	A	92
49 Opposites cards	I	95

Board games

Activity	Level*	Page
50 Board game 1: Clothes	E/I	97
51 Board game 2: Synonyms	I/A	98
52 Board game 3: Four of a kind	I/A	99
53 Board game 4: Three-in-a-row	I/A	100

Teacher-led activities

Activity	Level*	Page
54 Complete the sentences	E	106
55 Complete the story	I	108
56 Types of people	A	110
57 Missing words: Nouns	A	112
58 Words of similar meaning: Adjectives	A	114
59 Matching pairs: (Adjectives + nouns)	I	116
60 What does it mean? 1	A	118
61 What does it mean? 2	A	120
62 Word groups	A	122
63 The homophone game	I/A	123
64 The definition game	I	124
65 Word association	A	125
66 Carry on the story	All	62
67 Vocabulary sets cards	I	127

20-square activities

Activity	Level*	Page
Numbers 1–20		130
68 20-square 1: Word sets	E	131
69 20-square 2: Confusing words	I	132
70 20-square 3: Synonyms	I	133
71 20-square 4: Explain the words	A	134
72 20-square 5: Beginnings and endings	I	135
73 20-square 6: Ambiguous headlines	A	136
74 20-square 7: Explain the idiom	A	137

Miscellaneous activities

Activity	Level*	Page
75 The alphabet race	E	138
76 Word hunt	I	139
77 New words from old	A	140
78 Puzzle it out	I	141
79 Find the words	I	143
80 True or false 1	E/I	144
81 True or false 2	I/A	145
82 True or false 3	A	146
83 Make two words	I	147
84 Arrange the words	A	148
85 It's quiz time: Idioms	A	149
86 Verb + noun collocations	A	150
87 Sort out the text 1	I	151
88 Sort out the text 2	I	152
89 Sort out the punch lines	I/A	153
90 Who wrote what?	A	154

* E: elementary   I: intermediate   A: advanced   All

Introduction

Vocabulary Games and Activities is a source book for teachers, containing a collection of 90 activities for teaching and revising vocabulary. Most of them developed as a result of running a series of vocabulary learning courses in Sweden during the past ten years. They range from elementary to advanced activities, most of which contain material to be photocopied. It is hoped they will prove useful in general courses where vocabulary learning is at last beginning to play an important and active part.

The choice of lexical items in the book is largely subjective and has been chosen principally to illustrate a particular type of activity rather than imply that the words found here are more useful or important than other words. In choosing the vocabulary, quite a lot of material has been taken from the author's Test Your Vocabulary series (also published by Penguin Books). Activities invariably have to be changed or adapted to suit one's own particular group of students, so I hope teachers will feel free to make any changes they feel necessary. What is presented in **Vocabulary Games and Activities** is, above all, ideas which, hopefully, will stimulate and encourage teachers to devise their own activities based on these ideas.

I am sometimes asked why one should go to the trouble of photocopying and cutting out words for activities when the same thing could probably be done on a single sheet of paper. My answer is that although it is certainly more work for the teacher, the results are well worth it. Learning seems to become more active, the students get more involved and, in my experience, retention improves enormously. Once a student has done an exercise on paper, it feels "finished", and is never easy to repeat. By allowing the students to physically arrange words on a table (e.g. in matching pairs or group of words), the sense of touch is used, and the more senses that are involved in the learning process the better. The learning process is also made more dynamic and enjoyable by working with fellow-students, and most of the activities in this book are designed for pair work, group work and, occasionally, whole class activities.

Finally, having led a relatively isolated life in Northern Europe, it is difficult to know which ideas can be claimed as one's own and which are other people's. Where I have consciously used someone else's idea I have of course acknowledged this. In other cases where I have devised an activity which someone else can lay prior claim to (it *is* possible for two people to come up with the same idea quite independently), then I apologize and will gladly make the appropriate acknowledgement in future editions of this book.

The organisation of this book

The activities have been grouped into nine sections: *Ice-breaker activities, Bingo activities, Matching pairs activities, Crossword and word square activities, Word grouping activities, Pair work and board games, Teacher-led activities, 20-square activities* and *Miscellaneous activities*. Part 1 of the book gives detailed teacher's notes for each activity while Part 2 contains the various cards, hand-outs, etc. to be photocopied.

The material to be photocopied has been arranged in such a way that it also serves as an instant key to the majority of the activities. For example, in the matching pair activities the 20 words on the A sheet are in exactly the same places as the corresponding "matching word" on the B sheet. It is therefore important to remember to shuffle the cards prior to handing them out to the students. Where a key is not obvious from the layout, a separate key is included in the teacher's notes.

Classroom organisation

Although class sizes vary considerably, the book assumes an average class size of 10–20 students. Where possible, the classroom should be physically rearranged to facilitate working in pairs or groups. However, should this not be possible, even the more traditional front-facing rows of desks can be easily adapted for pair work and group work. For pair work, students can either work with the person sitting next to them or the person in front of or behind them. For group work, two students can easily turn their chairs round to face two others behind them. Where you have an uneven number of students in the class, most pair work activities can be done by three people (if necessary, two students against one).

The role of the teacher

Apart from the activities in the section *Teacher-led activities*, the teacher's role is largely a passive one. The teacher is mainly responsible for:

- preparing the material in sufficient quantities
- explaining clearly what is to be done
- "checking" answers at the end of an activity

Once an activity has started, students usually work independently of the teacher at their own pace. The teacher goes round the classroom listening and monitoring their progress and only interfering or helping if *absolutely necessary*.

Time limits

Although many teachers may disagree with me on this point, I strongly advise giving the class a time limit for most of the activities, and to stop them whether they have finished or not. Apart from the obvious difficulties of students finishing at different times, the checking process is often an integral and, from the learning point of view, important part of the activity. As such it is better that you check with the whole class rather than individual groups.

Storing the material

The material to be photocopied can be divided into two types: (a) hand-outs which the students write on, and (b) material which the students use but do not write on.

To save the teacher unnecessary work, therefore, it is a good idea that material that can be re-used is made as durable as possible. One way is to mount everything on thin card. (Many photocopiers nowadays allow the use of card.) These cards and hand-outs can then be stored in separate envelopes (clearly labelled on the outside) which can be handed back to the teacher at the end of the activity.

Nearly all the activities presented in this book require preparation on the part of the teacher. It is hoped that all the extra effort will prove to be rewarding.

Part 1 Teacher's notes

Ice-breaker activities

These activities are intended largely for fun – to be used with new groups to "break the ice" or when you have to divide the class into pairs or groups.

1 Find someone who...1 *Intermediate*

This is based on an activity that has been around for some time.

Method

1 Copy and cut up the cards on pages 24–7, so there is one for each student in the class.

2 Give out the cards and allow time for the students to work out which questions to ask.

3 Students now walk around the room trying to find answers to the five questions on their cards. To ensure that they talk to as many people as possible, tell them that they are only allowed to ask *one question* every time they talk to someone.

4 Students write down any answers to their questions, plus the name of the student who gave them the answer.

5 After a while, stop the activity, irrespective of whether everyone has found answers to all their questions.

6 As a quick follow-up, let each student read out one of the answers on his/her card. You might also take up any questions for which the students couldn't get answers.

2 Find someone who...2 *Elementary*

This is a variation of the above activity where, instead of the students getting individual cards, they all have a copy of the same hand-out.

Method

1 Give each student a copy of the hand-out on page 28.

2 As Activity 1, though students can now be allowed to ask two to three questions every time they talk to someone.

3 This time, you could go through all the questions, each student answering a different one.

3 Find someone who...3

Intermediate/Advanced

Method

As Activity 2. The hand-out is on page 29.

Activities for dividing a class into pairs/groups

The following activities can be used as ice-breakers or to divide a class into pairs (Activities 4–6) or groups of three or four (Activities 7–9).

4 Broken sentences 1 *Elementary*

In this activity students have to put together sentences which have been broken up into two halves.

Method

1 Copy and cut up the broken sentences on page 30, so there is one sentence for each pair of students in the class. (If there is an odd number, the teacher can take part.)

2 Students walk around the room trying to find their "pair". Once they have, they sit down.

3 Check by getting each pair to read out their sentence.

5 Broken sentences 2 *Intermediate*

Method

As Activity 4. The broken sentences are on page 31.

6 Broken proverbs *Advanced*

Method

As Activity 4, but with well-known proverbs. See page 32.

7 Broken sentences 3 *Intermediate*

In this activity students have to put together sentences which have been broken up into three parts.

Method

1 Copy and cut up the broken sentences on page 33, so there is one sentence for each group of three students in the class.

2 Students walk around the room trying to find their "group". Once they have, they sit down.

3 Check by getting each group to read out their sentence.

8 Word sets 1 *Intermediate/Advanced*

In this activity students have to find three words that are related to a particular heading (or key word).

Method

1 Copy and cut up the groups of four words on page 34, so there is one group of words for each group of four students in the class.

2 Students walk around the room trying to find their "group". Once they have, they sit down.

3 Check by getting each group to read out first the key word, then the three words related to it.

9 Word sets 2 *Advanced*

Method

As Activity 8. The word sets are on page 34.

Bingo activities

Although teachers may tire of bingo, students rarely do, and for sheer concentration there are few activities that can beat it. The activities described here are variations of bingo. For each activity there are ten different bingo cards. For larger classes, some students can work in pairs.

10 Picture bingo *Elementary*

The pictures chosen here are of 20 common objects found in the home.

Method

1 Copy and cut out the ten bingo cards on page 38. Also make two copies of the teacher's board on page 35. Leave one copy as it is but cut the other copy into 20 squares.

2 Give the students a card each. Allow a few minutes for them to look through them before beginning.

3 Put the 20 squares in a hat, cup, etc. Draw them out one at a time, saying each word as you do so and placing it on your "master board". If the students have the word (a picture on their cards), they cross it out.

4 Play proceeds until a student has crossed out every picture, in which case (s)he shouts *Bingo*!

5 Check by getting him/her to say which pictures (s)he has crossed out. (You can ask another student to monitor this, to avoid any cheating!)

11 Opposites bingo *Elementary*

In this game, the students have the opposites of the words the teacher reads out. (The students' words are given in brackets on the teacher's board.)

Method

As Activity 10. The student cards are on page 39 and the teacher's board is on page 35.

12 Prepositions bingo   *Intermediate*

The bingo cards here are slightly different than normal: each one consists of five sentences with missing prepositions. As each preposition is called out the students write them in the gaps on their cards. At the end of the game the winning student reads out all five sentences.

Method

As Activity 10, though it is a good idea to let the students read through the sentences first to know which prepositions to listen for. The student cards are on page 40 and the teacher's board is on page 36.

13 Synonyms bingo   *Intermediate*

In this game, the students have synonyms for the words the teacher reads out. (The students' words are given in brackets on the teacher's board.)

Method

As Activity 10. The student cards are on page 41 and the teacher's board is on page 36.

14 Definitions bingo   *Advanced*

In this game, the students have various words on their cards. The teacher reads out definitions of these words. (The students' words are given in brackets after the definitions on the teacher's board.) At the end of the game you can get the winning student to try to give a definition of each word on his/her card.

Method

As Activity 10. The student cards are on page 42 and the teacher's board is on page 37.

15 Parts of the body idioms bingo
Advanced

The bingo cards here each consist of five common idioms with gaps. Each gap represents a part of the body. To help the students, an explanation of the idiom is given in brackets after each sentence. As the parts of the body are called out the students write them in the gaps on their cards. As in Activity 12, at the end of the game the winning student reads out all five sentences.

Method

As Activity 10. The student cards are on page 43 and the teacher's board is on page 37.

Further suggestions

- Pictures of food, clothes, jobs, vehicles, buildings, tools, kitchen equipment, furniture, etc.
- Idioms of colour. As Activity 15, but this time a colour is left out of each sentence.
- Collective nouns. The teacher's board comprises phrases such as *a bunch of, a chest of,* etc. while the students have the missing nouns on their cards – *grapes, drawers,* etc.
- Phrasal verb bingo. The students have five sentences with a phrasal verb missing. The teacher's board has the missing phrasal verbs.
- Spelling bingo. The teacher spells out words and the students spell them back when checking.
- Phonetic bingo. Bingo cards consist of phonetics which the students have to match with the words they hear.
- Alphabet bingo. Very elementary: the bingo cards consist of letters of the alphabet.

Matching pairs activities

The activities in this section involve matching pairs of words in one way or another. All these activities are done in pairs or small groups. The items to be copied and cut up are arranged on two pages – A and B. This makes it easy for the teacher to see the correct solution. If coloured card or paper is available then different colours could be used for the A and B pages.

16 Verb + noun collocations

Elementary

In this activity the students have to pair up a verb (A words) with an appropriate noun (B words).

Method

1 Copy, cut up and *shuffle* sets of the cards on pages 44 and 45. Make enough sets for the class working in pairs or groups of three or four.

2 Give each group a set of A and B cards and tell them they have to arrange them into 20 pairs of words comprising a verb (on the left) and a noun (on the right).

3 Set a definite time limit and stop the students at the end of it, *whether they have finished or not.*

4 Check by going round the class from group to group. Each group reads out a pair in turn. The teacher says whether it is right or wrong. If right, it can be removed from the table (or turned over). The group gets 1 point for each correct answer. If wrong, the group gets no points and, without giving the correct answer, the teacher moves on to the next group.

5 Continue until all the pairs have been correctly read out.

17 Mini dialogues

Elementary

In this activity the students have to make two-line dialogues by matching up questions or sentences (A) with suitable responses (B).

Method

As Activity 16. The A questions and sentences are on page 46 and the B responses are on page 47.

18 Who uses what?

Intermediate

In this activity the students have to match up objects (A) with the people who use them (B).

Method

As Activity 16. The objects are on page 48 and the people who use them on page 49.

19 Definitions

Intermediate

In this activity the students have to match up words (A) with the correct definitions (B).

Method

As Activity 16. The words are on page 50 and the definitions on page 51.

20 Collective/partitive nouns

Intermediate/Advanced

In this activity the students have to match up collective and partitive nouns.

Method

As Activity 16. The A phrases (*a blade of...*, etc.) are on page 52 and the nouns on page 53.

21 Idioms

Advanced

In this activity the students have to combine verbs (A) with a noun phrase (B) to make 20 well-known idioms.

Method

As Activity 16. The verbs are on page 54 and the rest of the idiom on page 55. This time, as the pairs are read out you can give a bonus point to the group if they can either explain what the idiom means or put it in a sentence.

22 Funny definitions

Advanced

This final activity is largely for fun. The students have to match various words (A) with the correct (if somewhat unusual!) definitions (B).

Method

As Activity 16. The words are on page 56 and the definitions on page 57.

Acknowledgement: Excerpts from *Wordo Berzerko* by Ray Hand. Copyright © 1990 by Raymond V. Hand, Jr. Reprinted by permission of HarperCollins Publishers Inc.

Further suggestions

- Phrasal verbs: the phrasal verb in List A and the definition in List B. e.g.:

break down   stop working
carry on   continue

- Synonyms

- Opposites

- Jokes: the joke in List A and the punch line in List B. e.g.:

Doctor, I've got water on the knee.
Wear drainpipe trousers.

- Word association: each word in List A has an associated word in List B. e.g.:

bird   beak
tree   trunk

- Categories: three words have to be associated with the correct category. e.g.:

cup, plate, mug   CROCKERY
pigeon, sparrow, owl   BIRDS

Domino-type activities

These activities are based on the game dominoes and are played on a special board (see p. 58). Again the students work in pairs or groups. For ease of checking, the "dominoes" are arranged in the correct order on the page to be copied.

Acknowledgement: This is based on an idea from *Word Games With English Plus* © Deirdre Howard-Williams and Cynthia Herd 1989 – published by Heinemann English Language Teaching – Oxford.

23 Dominoes: Nouns 1   *Elementary*

In this activity, by combining the word on the right of each domino with the word on the left, 17 new words can be formed.

Method

1 Copy the board on page 58. Also copy, cut out and *shuffle* the dominoes on page 59. Make sure there are enough sets for the class working in pairs or groups of three or four.

2 Give each pair/group a board and a set of dominoes. Tell them to place the domino containing the words *room:coffee* on the board above *Start here*. Now tell them that they have to place the remainder of the dominoes on the board in such a way that 17 new words are formed by combining the right-hand word of one domino with the left-hand word of the one next to it.

3 Set a definite time limit and stop the students at the end of it, *whether they have finished or not*.

4 Check by beginning with the word *coffee:table*. Continue in a clockwise direction until you end with *bath:room*.

24 Dominoes: Nouns 2

Intermediate/Advanced

Method

As Activity 23. The dominoes for this activity are on page 59. Tell the students to start with the domino *pet:lady*.

25 Dominoes: Nouns 3   *Advanced*

Method

As Activity 23. The dominoes for this activity are on page 60. Tell the students to start with the domino *fall:dip*.

26 Dominoes: Clothes   *Elementary*

In this activity words have been broken up into two parts, of two to four letters each. The aim here is to form 17 words to do with clothes.

Method

As Activity 23. The dominoes for this activity are on page 60. Tell the students to start with the domino *at:glo*.

27 Dominoes: Phrasal verbs

Intermediate

In this activity a phrasal verb has to be matched to a definition.

Method

As Activity 23. The dominoes for this activity are on

page 61. Tell the students to begin with *quarrel:look into*.

28 Dominoes: Idioms   *Advanced*

In this activity an idiom (usually adjectival) has to be matched to a definition.

Method

As Activity 23. The dominoes for this activity are on page 61. Tell the students to begin with *inquisitive, curious:down-at-heel*.

Further suggestions

• Prepositions: match an adjective with a preposition. e.g.:

for: interested   in: typical

• Opposites

• Synonyms

• Prefixes and suffixes: complete words using a prefix or a suffix. e.g.:

taken:dis   appointed:in
ing:fashion   able:courage

29 Word association dominoes 1

Elementary

This is a freer, more open-ended variation of dominoes and is for groups of three or four students. (Alternatively it can be played by three or four teams with two students per team.) The aim is to find links or associations between pairs of words.

Method

1 Copy and cut out the 52 words (hereafter called cards) on page 62. Make sure there is one set for each group.

2 Arrange the class into groups of three or four. The students sit facing each other around a desk or table. Each group is given a set of cards.

3 It might be an idea the first time you try this activity to explain the rules by demonstrating with one of the groups. The rules are as follows:

   • The cards are shuffled and each student is dealt eight, which (s)he hides from the others. The remainder of the cards are placed face down on the table.

   • The top two cards from the "pack" are turned over and laid out on the table. e.g.:

   birds   birthday

   • Decide who starts. Play will then continue in a clockwise direction. Player 1 looks at his/her cards and tries to find one or two words that can be linked to or associated with either the word *birds* or *birthday*. If (s)he finds a link, (s)he places the new word or words next to the one on the table, at the same time explaining orally the link. Let us suppose the student has the word *money*, (s)he places it next to *birthday* and says, e.g. *I was given a lot of money on my birthday.* So now we have the following on the table:

   birds   birthday   money

   Of course, if the person also had the word *aunt* (s)he can get rid of two cards by saying: *I got money from my aunt on my birthday.*

   • The rest of the group now decide whether to accept or reject the association. (In the case of a dispute, the teacher's word is final!) If accepted, the word *money* is placed on top of *birthday* so that there are always only two cards showing. Play passes to the next player who now has to find associations for either *birds* or *money*. If the association is rejected, the student removes the word from the table and play passes on to the next person. Alternatively, if the player cannot make a link or association (s)he says *Pass*.

   • The first person to get rid of all his/her cards wins.

   • At any stage during the game a player may exchange one of his/her cards for a new one from the remaining cards in the pack. But this means forfeiting a turn!

4 Should the game go on too long, the teacher can say *Stop*, in which case the player with the least number of cards left is the winner.

30 Word association dominoes 2

Intermediate

Method

As Activity 29. The words to be cut out are on page 63.

31 Word association dominoes 3
Advanced

Method

As Activity 29. The words to be cut out are on page 64.

Crosswords and word square activities

Most students enjoy doing crosswords and word squares. The following activities take these a stage further by making them into communicative group activities. There are three type of activities, namely:

• half a crossword activities

• sort out the clues activities

• word battleships activities

Half a crossword activities

In these activities the students work in two groups of two to four students. One group is called A and the other B. Each group has an incomplete crossword. By asking for and giving definitions, they try to fill in the missing words.

Acknowledgement: Based on an idea in an article by Elizabeth Woodeson published in *Modern English Teacher* magazine, 1982, published by Modern English Publications.

32 Half a crossword: Sports, hobbies and pastimes
Elementary

In this crossword all the missing words are different sports, hobbies or pastimes.

Method

1 Copy and cut up the crosswords on page 65 (Group A) and page 66 (Group B).

2 Divide the class into A and B groups of between two and four students per group. They sit facing each other. Give each group the appropriate crossword and allow them time to check through the words they will need to define before starting. If necessary, give individual help at this stage.

NOTE: On no account must they allow the other group to see their crossword.

3 Explain that they have to take it in turns to ask for a word that is missing from their crossword. They simply ask: *What's 3 down? What's 14 across?*, etc. The other group now try to give as clear a definition as possible to help them guess the word.

4 Set a definite time limit and stop the students at the end of it, *whether they have finished or not.*

5 They can now compare crosswords and check any words they didn't fill in.

6 You can follow up by asking the groups to explain how they defined one or two words from the crossword.

33 Half a crossword: Jobs and occupations
Elementary

In this crossword all the missing words are different jobs and occupations.

Method

As Activity 32. The crosswords are on page 67 (Group A) and page 68 (Group B).

34 Half a crossword: Nouns
Intermediate

In this crossword all the missing words are different nouns.

Method

As Activity 32. The crosswords are on page 69 (Group A) and page 70 (Group B).

35 Half a crossword: Verbs
Intermediate/Advanced

In this crossword all the missing words are different verbs.

Method

As Activity 32. The crosswords are on page 71 (Group A) and page 72 (Group B).

36 Half a crossword: Adjectives to describe people
Intermediate

In this crossword all the missing words are adjectives that can be used to describe people.

Method

As Activity 32. The crosswords are on page 73 (Group A) and page 74 (Group B).

37 Half a crossword: Types of people
Advanced

In this crossword all the missing words are different types of people.

Method

As Activity 32. The crosswords are on page 75 (Group A) and page 76 (Group B).

Further suggestions

- Abstract nouns, e.g. *anxiety, compassion, relief*, etc.
- Adjectives to describe temporary states, moods and feelings, e.g. *hoarse, drunk, pregnant, unconscious*, etc.
- Verbs to do with movement, e.g. *trudge, stagger, crawl*, etc.
- Health words, e.g. *midwife, maternity ward, surgeon, mumps*, etc.
- Crime and punishment, e.g. *arson, manslaughter, arrest, bail*, etc.

Sort out the clues activity

This is really a disguised matching pairs exercise where the students, working in pairs or groups, have to match up the words in the filled-in crossword with an appropriate clue (usually a definition).

38 Sort out the clues
Intermediate

The words contained here are a mixture of verbs, nouns and adjectives. However, just as with the *Half a crossword* activities, these activities could just as easily concentrate on specific word groups, e.g. verbs, health words, crime and punishment, etc.

Method

1 Copy the filled-in crossword on page 77 and copy, cut out and *shuffle* the clues on page 78.

2 Give each pair/group a copy of the crossword and clues. They now have to sort out the clues in two columns – Across clues on the left and Down clues on the right. In addition they write in the box in front of each clue the appropriate reference: *1 down, 15 across*, etc.

3 Set a definite time limit and stop the students at the end of it, *whether they have finished or not*.

4 Check by asking the groups in turn, e.g. *What's the clue for 2 across – BARGE?*, etc.

5 An additional follow-up would be to ask the students to turn over their crosswords, read out the definitions and see which group remembers which word it referred to.

Key (order as in hand-out on page 79)

10 across, 9 down, 16 down, 3 down, 23 across, 22 across, 25 down, 4 down, 12 across, 13 down, 18 down, 24 across, 1 down, 17 across, 15 across, 14 down, 20 across, 21 down, 2 across, 5 across, 6 across, 7 down, 19 across, 11 down, 8 across

Word battleships activities

This is a variation of the common word square activity. It is combined with the popular children's game of battleships. As in *Half a crossword* the students work in two groups of two to four. Each group has to find ten words which have been hidden in a 12 x 12 grid. Clues are provided to give them an idea of the sort of words they are looking for.

39 Word battleships 1 *Elementary*

Method

1 Copy the hand-outs on page 79 for Group A and page 80 for group B.

2 Arrange the class into A and B groups and give each group the appropriate hand-out. Allow a few minutes for them to look through it before they start.

3 Explain that they have to find ten words that are hidden in the grid. The clues next to the grid will tell them what sort of words they are looking for, e.g. two vegetables, two jobs, etc. They do this by asking for the contents of a particular square, which may contain a letter. To speed up the activity each group is allowed to ask for four squares each turn. If, during their turn, the groups think they know what a particular word is, they can say, e.g. *We think the word from 2B–2E is plum,* etc. If correct, they can fill in the letters without missing any turns. The first group to find all the words is the winner.

4 Set a definite time limit and stop the students at the end of it, *whether they have finished or not.*

5 Finally, let the groups compare their hand-outs to see which words, if any, they missed.

40 Word battleships 2 *Intermediate*

Method

As Activity 39. The hand-outs are on page 81 (Group A) and on page 82 (Group B).

41 Word battleships 3 *Advanced*

Method

As Activity 39. The hand-outs are on page 83 (Group A) and on page 84 (Group B).

Word grouping activities

Arranging words into groups or families is an excellent way of learning and/or reinforcing vocabulary.

42 Word groups 1: Nouns *Elementary*

This and all the other activities in this section are meant to be done in groups of three to five students.

Method

1 Copy, cut out and *shuffle* the words on page 85. Make sure you have one set per group.

2 Arrange the class into groups. Give each group a set of words and tell them they have to place five words under each heading. (They will need a desk or table on which to work.)

3 Set a definite time limit and stop the students at the end of it, *whether they have finished or not.*

4 Instead of just reading out the correct answers at the end, you might like to try the following:

- Ask one group to tell you which words they have placed under *IN THE KITCHEN.* If they didn't get them all right, tell them which words are correct, e.g. *You got three right – cooker, fridge and kettle.* Move on to the next group and ask them if they can say what the missing two words are. Continue in this way until all five words are given. (In the unlikely event that after going round the class you still haven't found five correct words, tell them the answer.)

- Continue in this way with the remaining four groups. (By using this method of checking, it allows the groups to "change their minds" and reshuffle their cards during the checking stage.)

43 Word groups 2: Nouns

Intermediate

Method

As Activity 42. The words to be cut up are on page 86.

44 Word groups 3: Adjectives

Intermediate/Advanced

Method

As Activity 42. The words to be cut up are on page 87.

45 Word groups 4: Verbs   *Advanced*

Method

As Activity 42. The words to be cut up are on page 88.

46 Word groups 5: Idioms, etc.

Advanced

This is slightly different from Activities 42–45. Here the students have to put the words and phrases into eight groups of three words and suggest a possible heading for each group. (Usually two of the three words or phrases in each group are idioms.)

Method

As Activity 42. The words to be cut up are on page 89.

Key (suggestion)

FEAR
hair-raising, have kittens, petrified
ANGER
fly off the handle, hit the roof, irate
VANITY
big-headed, blow one's own trumpet, conceited
MEMORY/FORGETFULNESS
slip one's mind, have a memory like a sieve, amnesia
MADNESS/INSANITY
crazy, have a screw loose, off one's head

LOSS OF JOB/UNEMPLOYMENT
get the sack, on the dole, made redundant
SPEECH/SPEAKING
garrulous, have the gift of the gab, hold one's tongue
MONEY/LACK OF MONEY
hard up, in the red, make ends meet

Pair work cards and board games

Pair work cards

The following three activities are for pairs of students. They are a simple but effective way of both teaching and testing vocabulary.

47 Definitions cards 1: Nouns

Advanced

There are five cards altogether. Each card has a front (A) and a back (B). On the front are definitions of eight words (in this case nouns), while on the back are the words being defined. So there are 40 words to learn/test altogether.

Method

1 Copy and cut up the five cards on pages 90–2, so there is one set for each group of ten students in the class. Fold each copy and stick it together so that the words and definitions are back to back. (To prevent the problem of the words or definitions shining through the paper, they could be stuck onto either side of a piece of card instead.)

2 Divide the students into pairs. One set of cards is sufficient for ten students, i.e. five pairs. (If there are more than ten students you will need further sets of cards.)

3 Give each pair one of the cards. (It doesn't matter in which order they get them.) They work on this card for a while and then at a signal from the teacher to *Change!* the cards are rotated. To avoid a mix-up, rotate the cards in the same direction every time. This continues until each of the pairs has had all five cards.

4 The basic method of working with each card is as follows:

• When they get a card they first of all make a note of its number on a piece of paper (This is to avoid getting the same card twice!)

• The person with the definitions – the one with the A side of the card – starts first. (S)he goes through all the definitions, one after the other, asking each time, e.g. *What's the word for a way of pronouncing a language, particular to one area?* After each definition is a number in brackets. This refers to the number of the correct answer on the other side, in this case word number 7. After asking the question, the partner looks at the eight words on his/her side of the card and gives an answer, guessing if necessary, e.g. *It's Word Number 7. It's 'accent'.* The first person now says if it is right or wrong. If wrong, (s)he can say: *No, it's Word Number ...* whatever number is in brackets.

• When all eight words have been gone through in this way, the pairs change over. This time the person with the B side of the card starts. (S)he goes through the words one after the other, saying, e.g. *Give a definition of the word 'bait'.* The partner will now (hopefully) answer: *It's Definition Number 4. It's food used to attract fish or animals so that they can be caught.*

5 As a quick follow-up, read out one or two definitions from each card and see how many of the students can remember the words. (The results are often surprisingly good!)

48 Definitions cards 2: Verbs
Advanced

This time each word is a definition of a verb. There are 40 verbs altogether.

Method
As Activity 47. The cards to be cut out are on pages 92–4.

49 Opposites cards
Intermediate

These cards teach or test opposites. Each card has six words, so altogether there are 30 opposites.

Method
As Activity 47. The cards to be cut out are on pages 95–6. The main difference here is that the students have to answer by giving the *opposite* of the word they can see. (At the beginning there is a tendency for them to read out the word they see rather than give the opposite of it.) To help them, the first letter of the opposite is given.

Further suggestions
• Synonyms
• Phrasal verbs
• Idioms (definitions), etc.

Board games

Most students like board games and the first three are for pairs, which also require dice.

50 Board game 1: Clothes
Elementary/Intermediate

In this game, the board contains 30 drawings of clothes which the students, working in pairs, have to match with the words in the boxes below.

Method
1 Give each pair a copy of the board on page 97. They will also need a die, and it might be easier if they work with different coloured pens or pencils.

2 Player 1 throws the die, e.g. (s)he throws 5. (S)he looks at the words in Box 5, chooses one, and writes it down under the appropriate drawing. At the same time (s)he crosses out the word from the list. Play now passes on to Player 2 who does the same.

3 Play continues in this way. Should a player throw a number where all the words have been used up, (s)he misses a turn. Likewise, should a player be unable to place a word (because they don't know

it), (s)he "passes" and play moves to his/her partner.

4 Set a time limit and stop the students at the end of it. The teacher can read out the answers and the students can check. They score 1 point for every word placed correctly and lose 1 point for every word placed incorrectly.

Key (from left to right)

cardigan, boots, nightdress, belt, bow tie
blouse, pyjamas, dressing gown, socks, suit
tights, apron, tie, jeans, shoes
skirt, T-shirt, waistcoat, jumper, overalls
coat, scarf, shirt, jacket, trousers
gloves, hat, dress, raincoat, vest

51 Board game 2: Synonyms

Intermediate/Advanced

In this game, the board contains 30 words which the students, working in pairs, have to match with the list of synonyms below the board.

Method

As Activity 50. The board is on page 98.

Key (from left to right)

idolize, astound, climb, aid, forbid
quarrel, construct, end, swindle, grasp
contemplate, loiter, loathe, exhibit, thrash
prosper, compel, predict, glisten, connect
leap, ridicule, loot, shake, respond
revolve, frighten, scamper, yell, commence

52 Board game 3: Four of a kind

Intermediate/Advanced

In this game, the board contains 30 groups of three words. The three words are related in some way. Below the board are boxes with additional words. The students, working in pairs, have to match these words with each group of three, adding one word to each group.

Method

As Activity 50. The board is on page 99.

Key (from left to right)

zinc, yew, trunk, gnat, hem
haddock, trawler, vagrant, madam (palindrome),
  circle
mansion, magpie, lizard, shoal, badger

rye, perjury, poppy, tangerine, rake
mint, veal, grater, clutch, crayfish
chisel, turnip, congregation, adolescent, famine

Further suggestions

• British–American English

• Opposites

• Drawings: furniture, parts of a car, tools, food, etc.

• Prepositions: interested ____, famous ____, etc.

53 Board game 4: Three-in-a-row

Intermediate/Advanced

The following activity is really a vocabulary quiz game for two or three teams of two students plus a question-master. It can be useful as an end-of-term fun activity.

Method

1 Copy the board for Three-in-a-Row on page 100. There should be one board per game. Also copy the questions on pages 101–5. Again there should be one set of questions per game.

2 Divide the class into groups of two or three teams, each with a question-master. Each group gets a board and each question-master gets a set of questions. In addition, each group is given a letter (A–C).

3 Decide which group is to begin. Play then continues in a clockwise direction.

4 The first group ask for a question by choosing a number 1–30, e.g. 30. The question-master then looks at the questions for Q30 and chooses one to ask the group. (There are six possible questions per number.) If correct, they write their letter (A–C) in the numbered square on the board. If incorrect, the question-master gives the answer and makes a note that this question has been asked.

5 Play continues in this way. The aim is for one group to "capture" *three adjacent squares* – either vertically, horizontally or diagonally.

6 Since there are six questions per square it will take the group quite some time to know every answer, so the game can be played quite often without the students becoming bored.

A variation on the above game is to have the teacher act as question-master with the class being divided into three teams A–C. This time, each team (and teacher) is given a board on which to mark not only their letter but also the other groups' letters. (Otherwise it would be difficult to check who has won, which squares are still free, etc.)

Teacher-led activities

In the previous activities in this book the teacher's role has been a somewhat passive one. His/her job has largely been to organize, set up and close an activity, with the students working for most of the time on their own in pairs or small groups.

In the following activities, however, the teacher has a more central (and traditional) role. As before, the students work mainly in pairs and small groups.

54 Complete the sentences

Elementary

In this activity, the students are given some cut-up words. They listen to sentences where a word (or words) has been left out, and suggest which word (or words) from their selection best completes each gap. They can either work alone or in pairs.

Method

1 Copy and cut up the words on page 106. The first 20 words are the words that are missing from the sentences, while the remaining words are distractors.

2 The students work either alone or in pairs. The words are divided up amongst each student/pair. Make sure that everyone has at least one correct word and, depending on the number of students in the class, one distractor. All the words are placed face up on the table or desk.

3 Read out the sentences on page 107, one at a time. If necessary, read each sentence more than once.

Make sure you clearly indicate (by making a sound, etc.) where the missing word is in each sentence.

4 The student who thinks (s)he has the missing word, holds it up and says it out loud. If correct, the word is turned face down. This helps the teacher to see how many words each student has left.

5 If incorrect, the teacher can ask other students to suggest the missing word. (They may be able to guess it even if it isn't one of their words.) Further help can be given, e.g. *It starts with the letter p.* Again, if the teacher is close enough to the students (s)he may be able to point to a student/pair and say *It's one of your words!*

6 Continue until all 20 sentences have been completed successfully.

NOTE: Although this exercise can be done as a simple paper/pen exercise, there is a 100 per cent increase in concentration by doing it this way. Students listen eagerly to each sentence, and apart from testing to see if they can see if a word fits into a particular context, it also gives good practice in seeing when a word doesn't fit (an equally useful skill to learn).

55 Complete the story

Intermediate

This is similar to Activity 54, but this time instead of reading out isolated sentences, the teacher reads a complete story with 24 gaps. Again, the students are given more words than are actually missing from the story.

Method

As Activity 54. The words to be cut up are on page 108 (first the 24 missing words, then 24 distractors). The story to be read out is on page 109.

56 Types of people

Advanced

In this activity the teacher reads out 16 definitions of people. The students listen and try to match the definition with the words they have been given. The students can work in pairs or groups of three.

Method

1 Copy the hand-out on page 110 and give each pair/group a copy.

2 Read out the sentences on page 111, one by one. Allow the students time to write down their answers.

3 Check orally.

4 As a follow-up, get the students to turn over their papers and read out the definitions again (in a different order) to see how many words they remember.

Further suggestions

- crime and punishment
- health words
- adjectives to describe people
- business English

57 Missing words: Nouns   *Advanced*

This, and the following five activities, are for advanced groups. Using them as examples, it shouldn't be too difficult to construct activities for lower-level groups.

In this activity, the teacher writes words on the board and the students match them with sentences which have missing words. As usual they work in pairs or groups.

Method

1 Copy the hand-out on page 112 and give each pair/group a copy.

2 Copy, cut out and *shuffle* the words on page 113. Place them face down in front of you on the table.

3 Take the top word, and write it on the board. Allow the students about a minute to decide which sentence it is missing from. Then rub out the word, pick up the next one, and write that on the board instead.

4 Continue in this way until all the words have been read out.

5 Check orally.

58 Words of similar meaning: Adjectives   *Advanced*

In this activity, the students have to find an adjective from the 16 they are given which is similar to three others. As usual they work in pairs or groups.

Method

As Activity 57. The hand-out is on page 114 and the adjectives to be cut up are on page 115.

59 Matching pairs: (Adjective + noun)   *Intermediate*

This activity concentrates on adjective + noun collocations. As usual the students work in pairs or groups. (This activity is only partly teacher-led.)

Method

1 Copy the hand-out on page 116 and divide the class into four or five groups. Give each group a hand-out.

2 Copy, cut up and *shuffle* the 25 words on page 117. (NOTE: The last five words are distractors.)

3 Give each group five words. Tell them to see if they can complete some of the 20 phrases with these words. Explain that they will receive 25 words altogether – in other words, five words will *not* be used.

4 After three or four minutes, get the students to pass the words along from group to group in a clockwise direction.

5 Continue in this way until every group has seen every word.

6 Check orally.

60 What does it mean? 1   *Advanced*

This activity tests the students' knowledge of idioms. As usual they work in pairs or groups.

Method

1 Copy the hand-out on page 118 and give each pair/group a copy.

2 Read out the sentences on page 119. Allow a minute or so after each one for the students to write the number of the sentence next to the idiom with the same meaning.

3 Check orally.

61 What does it mean? 2   *Advanced*

Sixteen further idioms.

Method

As Activity 57. The student's hand-out is on page 120 and the teacher's sentences are on page 121.

---

62 Word groups   Advanced

This activity is similar to Activities 42–6, but this time is teacher-led. Before starting, divide the class into four groups.

Method

1 Copy, cut out and *shuffle* the words on page 122. Place them in a pile face down on the table in front of you.

2 Write the following headings on the board. Allow enough room to write five words under each heading.

Ways of looking	*Ways of moving*
Expressing dislike	*Speaking and listening*
Facial gestures	*Animal sounds*

3 In turns one person from each group comes to the front, takes the top word, looks at it and tries to place it under the correct heading. (No one is allowed to shout out the answer!)

4 If correct, the group gain 1 point. If incorrect, the word is rubbed out and placed at the bottom of the pile to be used later on.

5 Continue until all the words have been placed correctly.

6 The group with the highest number of points is the winner.

---

63 The homophone game

Intermediate/Advanced

This activity is for pairs or groups. Before starting explain what homophones are, namely words that sound the same but have different meanings and spellings, e.g. *I, eye.*

Method

1 On page 123 are two lists of suitable homophones that can be used for this activity. List 2 is more difficult than List 1.

2 Before starting tell each pair/group to write the numbers 1–20 in a column on a separate piece of paper.

3 Read out the words one at a time. After you have read out each word, allow the pairs/groups approximately 30–40 seconds to try to write down two possible words.

4 Continue in this manner until all 20 words have been read out.

5 Check orally. If you wish, get one person from each pair/group to write their answer on the board. Try to get them to explain the different meanings.

---

64 The definition game   Intermediate

This activity tests the students' ability to define words. Before starting, the class is divided into four groups, A–D.

Method

1 Copy, cut out and *shuffle* the 20 words on page 124. Place them face down in front of you.

2 Group A starts. One person from the group comes out to the front of the class. (S)he picks up the top word and tries to give a definition of it so that his/her group can guess what the word is. If they do, they keep the word. If not, one of the other groups is allowed to guess and thus gain an extra word. If no one guesses, the word can ether be placed at the bottom (and used later on) or the teacher tells the class what the word is.

3 Continue in this manner. The group with the most words at the end wins.

---

65 Word association   Advanced

This activity tests the students' ability to see links or associations between pairs of words. Before starting, the class is divided into four groups, A–D.

Method

1 Copy, cut out and *shuffle* the 20 words (called student cards) on page 125. Divide them up amongst the four groups. Tell them to lay them face up in front of them.

2 Copy, cut up and *shuffle* the 20 words (called teacher's cards) on page 126. Lay them face down in front of you.

3 Hold up and read out the first teacher's card. Ask the groups if anyone thinks they have a card that is linked with this one. If so, they hold it up and say

Teacher's notes

it out loud and explain the link or association. If correct, they turn the card face down. If incorrect, go on to the next word.

4 Continue until all 20 words have been correctly associated.

66 Carry on the story   *All*

This is an activity for the whole class, using the same words as those used in *Word association dominoes* (Activities 29–31). Before starting, divide the class into four groups, A–D. One person in each group will keep the score.

Method

1 Copy, cut out and *shuffle* the words, e.g. the elementary set of words on page 62. Place them face down on the table in front of you.

2 Take the top three cards and write them on the board, e.g.:

football   school   family

Explain that the aim of the activity is to make up a story, working together as a class.

3 Group A begins. One person in the group starts the story. It can be about anything, but the person can't stop talking until (s)he uses one or more of the words on the board. In order to know when the person has finished, (s)he says *Pass* and the next group continues.

Every word used scores 1 point, so in any one turn a group can gain 1–3 points. Using the above words, the person might say, for example, *I was walking home from **school** one day when I decided to have a game of **football** with my friends. Pass.* (2 points scored.)

4 Play now passes to Group B. Before they start, the teacher wipes out any words used, takes new ones from the pack and writes these on the board, e.g.:

family   job   film

NOTE: There should always be three words on the board at any one time.

5 Try to repeat the last sentence (or occasionally summarize the story) as you move from group to group, so the main idea of the story is kept alive.

6 The group with the highest number of points at the end wins.

NOTE: Try to make sure that a different person in the group speaks each time, although you can allow the group to confer, if the person seems to be having difficulty.

67 Vocabulary sets cards   *Intermediate*

This activity is useful to test specific areas of vocabulary. Before starting, divide the class into five groups of two to four students.

Method

1 Copy and cut out the five cards on pages 127–9.

2 Appoint a group secretary who will be responsible for recording the group's answers.

3 Give each group one of the cards. Tell the secretary to make a note of the card number and the heading on a separate piece of paper. Tell him/her to also write down the numbers 1–10 under the heading. This is where the group will record their answers. *They must not write on the actual cards!*

4 Give them a time limit, e.g. five minutes, in which they have to find out and write down the missing words in the ten sentences.

5 When the time is up, tell them to stop. Pass the cards from group to group in a clockwise direction. Again, remind them to write down the card number and heading, followed by the numbers 1–10 before they start.

6 Continue in this manner until everyone has had all five cards. Collect the cards before checking the answers.

7 Check orally. Start with *Card 1: Describing personality*. Tell them all to look at their answers for this card. By now, there will be an element of suspense and anticipation in the classroom because all they have in front of them are various words. Few will remember the original sentences, so it makes checking all the more exciting.

Ask each group for their answer to Sentence 1. *Then* read out the context sentence to remind them. Award one point for every correct word. Continue in the same way with the remaining sentences.

8 Continue in this manner with Cards 2–4.

16

Key

Card 1: Describing personality

1 *imaginative* 2 *ambitious* 3 *moody* 4 *immature*
5 *jealous* 6 *sociable* 7 *big-headed* 8 *punctual*
9 *impatient* 10 *easy-going*

Card 2: Cars and motoring

1 *clutch, brake, accelerator* 2 *handbrake* 3 *overtake*
4 *driving licence* 5 *lanes* 6 *speed limit* 7 *seatbelt*
8 *service stations* 9 *boot* 10 *bypass*

Card 3: House and home

1 *wallpaper* 2 *central heating* 3 *basement* 4 *micro-wave oven* 5 *letterbox* 6 *chimney* 7 *blinds* 8 *block of flats* 9 *French windows* 10 *mortgage*

Card 4: Books, etc.

1 *catalogue* 2 *diary* 3 *novel* 4 *manual* 5 *brochure*
6 *directory* 7 *dictionary* 8 *phrase book* 9 *encyclopedia* 10 *magazines*

Card 5: Education

1 *subjects* 2 *staff* 3 *compulsory* 4 *headteacher/headmaster/headmistress* 5 *university* 6 *terms*
7 *time-table* 8 *boarding* 9 *primary* 10 *secondary*

20-square activities

Activities 68–74 are all based on a board containing 20 squares. They are also all for students working in groups.

68 20-square 1: Word sets *Elementary*

In this activity students have to find a word to add to three other words. Before starting, the class is divided into four groups, A–D.

Method

1 Copy the hand-out on page 131. Make sure there are enough copies for each group. (If the groups are large, have one copy for every two or three students.) Also copy, cut out and *shuffle* the numbers 1–20 on page 130 and place them face down in front of you.

2 Give out the hand-outs. Decide which group will start (e.g. Group A). The game then continues in a clockwise direction.

3 Hold up the first number (e.g. 5). The first group look at square number 5 on the hand-out and try to think of another word that will go with the three there. In this case, they would have to think of another vegetable, e.g. *potato*.

4 If correct, everyone puts a cross through this square and writes in the letter of the group that gave the correct answer – in this case they would write *A* in the square.

5 If incorrect, the number is put at the bottom of the pack to be used later on in the game.

6 Play continues in this way. The team with the highest number of "squares" at the end is the winner.

NOTE: The reason for using the number cards is that it creats a certain amount of suspense – no one knows which square is going to be next. This results in heightened attention.

69 20-square 2: Confusing words

Intermediate

In this activity students have to explain the differences between pairs of words which are often confused. Before starting, the class is divided into four groups.

Method

As Activity 68. The hand-out is on page 132 and the numbers 1–20 on page 130.

70 20-square 3: Synonyms

Intermediate

This activity tests the students' knowledge of synonyms. To help, some letters from the answer are given. Before starting, the class is divided into four groups.

Method

As Activity 68. The hand-out is on page 133 and the numbers 1–20 on page 130.

Key

1 *enormous* 2 *insane* 3 *vanish* 4 *scared* 5 *wealthy*
6 *stubborn* 7 *boast* 8 *dreadful* 9 *peculiar* 10 *rude*
11 *permit* 12 *giddy* 13 *eager* 14 *marvellous*
15 *change* 16 *reliable* 17 *wicked* 18 *irritated*
19 *select* 20 *industrious*

71 20-square 4: Explain the words

Advanced

In this activity students have to try to explain the meaning of various words. The words are part of a phrase and are shown in italics.

Method

As Activity 68. The hand-out is on page 134 and the numbers 1–20 on page 130.

72 20-square 5: Beginnings and endings

Intermediate

In this activity students have to try to make words which start with or end with various letters. The method this time is slightly different.

Method

1 As Activity 68 (Steps 1–2). The hand-out is on page 135 and the numbers 1–20 on page 130.

2 Hold up the first number (e.g. 4). The first group look at square number 4 and try to think of a word that starts with the letters *sh*, e.g. *shirt*.

3 If correct, the group get one point and play passes to the remaining groups who also try to think of a word beginning with *sh*. Again, if they do they gain one point. When all four groups have tried, every-one crosses out this square. (To avoid cheating, the teacher can keep score on the board.)

4 Play continues in this way. The team with the highest number of points at the end is the winner.

73 20-square 6: Ambiguous headlines

Advanced

In this activity students have to try to explain the two possible meanings of the various headlines.

Method

As Activity 68 The hand-out is on page 136 and the numbers 1–20 on page 130.

74 20-square 7: Explain the idiom

Advanced

In this activity students have to try to explain the meaing of various idioms. Again, for a change, a different method can be used.

Method

1 As usual the groups are given a copy of the hand-out on page 137, but this time the numbers 1–20 *are not used*.

2 One group starts, e.g. Group A. They themselves choose a square and ask Group B to explain the idiom in that square. (If groups are wise, they will choose squares containing idioms they themselves are not confident of answering.)

3 As Activity 68 (Steps 3–6).

Miscellaneous activities

The remaining activities in the book don't fit easily into any of the previous categories and consist largely of various hand-outs, mostly at intermediate or advanced level.

75 The alphabet race

Elementary

This is a simple activity to give students practice in using the alphabet. (Useful for students whose first language uses a different alphabet.) Before starting, divide the class into pairs or groups of three.

Method

1 Copy the hand-out on page 138 and give one copy to each pair/group.

2 Set a time limit, e.g. five minutes. When everyone is ready, tell them to begin. After five minutes tell them to stop.

3 Check orally.

Key

1 *N* 2 *T* 3 *day, dog, etc.* 4 *goat* 5 *six* 6 *coat, boat, etc.* 7 *O, I and E* 8 *T* 9 *E* 10 *I, N, T and E (twice)* 11 *I* 12 *J* 13 *carrot, comb, cotton, crab, cream* 14 *R* 15 *cap, apple, etc.*

Acknowledgement: This is based on an idea from *Verbal Reasoning for 10 to 12 Year Olds* by Robin Brown, Hodder & Stoughton Educational 1991, p. 6.

---

76 Word hunt   Intermediate

This is an open-ended activity. Students can either work individually, in pairs or in small groups.

Method

Give everyone a copy of the hand-out on page 139. Set a time limit and check answers orally. Alternatively, if working individually, they can get together with one or more students and compare answers.

---

77 New words from old   Advanced

In this activity, students make words by adding one word to another, either before or after it. The new words formed are either single nouns or two-word nouns. It can be done in pairs or small groups.

Method

1 Copy the hand-out on page 140 and give one copy to each pair/group.

2 Set a time limit. Check answers orally.

Key

1 *arm* 2 *book* 3 *card* 4 *coat* 5 *horse* 6 *light* 7 *paper* 8 *ship* 9 *water* 10 *ball* 11 *room* 12 *chair* 13 *house* 14 *post* 15 *sun* 16 *board* 17 *head* 18 *line* 19 *table* 20 *boy* 21 *man* 22 *step* 23 *box* 24 *pot* 25 *hair*

---

78 Puzzle it out   Intermediate

This is a problem-solving activity for groups of three to five students.

Method

1 Copy the hand-out on page 141, and give one copy to each group. Copy and cut out the clues on page 142. Again, give one set to each group.

2 Explain that there are five people staying at a hotel: Mr Petty, Mr Grove, Mrs Williams, Ms Stevens and Mr Harvey. Using the clues, the students have to complete the missing information in the table, namely each person's job, character, interest or hobby, plus one other item of information. Set a time limit and check orally.

Key

Room 101 – Mr Grove – traffic warden – sociable – gardening – is a twin
Room 102 – Ms Stevens – surgeon – optimistic – painting – is Australian
Room 103 – Mr Petty – plumber – conceited – amateur dramatics – is bald
Room 104 – Mrs Williams – solicitor – mean – tennis – is bilingual
Room 105 – Mr Harvey – estate agent – bossy – bird-watching – is a widower

Acknowledgement: This is based on an idea from *Keep Talking* by Friederike Klippel, Cambridge University Press 1984, p.181.

---

79 Find the words   Intermediate

This is a useful activity for guessing vocabulary in context. It can be done in pairs or small groups.

Method

1 Copy out the hand-out on page 143 and give one copy to each pair/group.

2 Set a time limit. Check orally.

Key (suggestion)

1 *shop* 2 *night* 3 *through* 4 *time* 5 *hours* 6 *found* 7 *from* 8 *home* 9 *when* 10 *same* 11 *decided* 12 *police*

Acknowledgement: Activities based on an idea from, Ruth Gairns and Stuart Redman, *Working With Words*, 1986, Cambridge University Press.

---

80 True or False 1   Elementary/Intermediate

This is a betting game for pairs or small groups.

Method

1 Copy the hand-out on page 144 and give one copy to each pair/group.

2 Explain the rules, namely that for each statement they put a tick in the true or false box and then bet

10–100 points on their answer being correct. They write the number of points in the *Bet* column.

3 Set a time-limit and check orally. To avoid cheating, let the students mark one another's hand-outs.

4 Each answer will either be correct or incorrect. If correct, they gain the number of points they bet. If incorrect, they lose the number of points they bet. (Students copy the amount under *Bet* to the *Gain* or *Loss* column.)

5 At the end, add up the total losses and gains to arrive at a grand total, which is gains minus losses.

6 The pair/group with the highest score wins.

Key

1 *T* 2 *F* 3 *F* 4 *T* 5 *F* 6 *F* 7 *T* 8 *F* 9 *F* 10 *F* 11 *T*
12 *F* 13 *T* 14 *T* 15 *F*

Acknowledgement: This is a variation on an activity which I first saw demonstrated by Mario Rinvolucri at a workshop in Malmö, Sweden.

81 True or False 2   *Intermediate/Advanced*

Method

As Activity 77. The hand-out is on page 145.

Key

1 *T* 2 *F* 3 *F* 4 *T* 5 *F* 6 *T* 7 *T* 8 *F* 9 *F* 10 *T* 11 *F*
12 *T* 13 *F* 14 *F* 15 *T*

82 True or False 3   *Advanced*

Method

As Activity 77. The hand-out is on page 146.

Key

1 *F* 2 *T* 3 *T* 4 *F* 5 *F* 6 *T* 7 *T* 8 *F* 9 *T* 10 *F* 11 *T*
12 *F* 13 *T* 14 *T* 15 *F*

83 Make two words   *Intermediate*

In this activity the letters which form the end of one word also form the beginning of another word. The students work in pairs or small groups.

Method

1 Copy, cut out and *shuffle* the words on page 147. Give one set to each pair/group.

2 Tell the students that they have to arrange the words in three columns, so that two words can be formed. Demonstrate with the following:

blou   se   cret
(*blouse/secret*)

3 Set a time limit, and then check orally, taking one pair from each group.

84 Arrange the words   *Advanced*

This is a useful activity where the students have to group words under headings – in this case whether certain adjectives describe people's good qualities, faults or either. (Different cultures often have different ideas on what are positive or negative qualities.) Students can work individually or in pairs.

Method

1 Give everyone a copy of the hand-out on page 148.

2 Set a time limit, and check orally. Encourage discussion, especially where the students disagree over a word.

Further suggestions

• List of words to do with taste. Arrange into pleasant and unpleasant tastes.

• List of words to do with sound. Arrange into pleasant and unpleasant sounds, or loud and quiet ones.

• List of words to do with movement. Arrange into quick and slow movements.

85 It's quiz time: Idioms   *Advanced*

This is a fun activity for advanced groups which tests their knowledge of idioms. Students work in pairs or small groups.

Method

1 Give each pair/group a copy of the hand-out on page 149. (Tell them to write their answers on a separate piece of paper.)

2 Set a time limit. Encourage them to guess when they really have no idea of the answer.

3 Check orally.

Key (suggestion)

1 *A party for men only which is usually held before a wedding.*
2 *You would share the cost of the meal.*
3 *He has died.*
4 *The neck.*
5 *He is in prison.*
6 *Depressed, miserable.*
7 *Naked.*
8 *A very good relationship.*
9 *Because they carry on working during a strike.*
10 *He has been given a large payment to leave the company he works for.*
11 *On the face. (They are the wrinkles you get at the corner of your eyes.)*
12 *You would be ignoring him or her.*
13 *(S)he turns up at a party without being invited.*
14 *Very lively.*
15 *You would be asleep.*
16 *A holiday spent doing one's usual work.*
17 *You set the date of your wedding.*
18 *Someone who gets up early.*
19 *It describes a third person who stays in the company of two lovers although they want to be alone.*
20 *The local newspaper.*

Further suggestions

You can make similar quizzes for:

• phrasal verbs (Why is it usually only men who are *called up*?)

• crime words (What does *an arsonist* like doing?)

• health words (Why would a woman be in the *maternity ward* of a hospital?)

• food words (What colour is *celery*?)

• business words (When would you usually give someone an *invoice*?)

86 Verb + noun collocations

Advanced

In this activity, the students have to match verbs with various nouns. The nouns are ones that typically follow certain verbs.

Method

1 Give each student/pair a copy of the hand-out on page 150.

2 Explain what is to be done and check orally.

Key

ask	*permission, the way*
break	*one's leg, the ice*
catch	*a cold, fire*
change	*gear, one's mind*
cut	*a tooth, corners*
draw	*a conclusion, the curtains*
give	*thanks, the impression*
hold	*the fort, the line*
lay	*a trap for someone, the table*
lose	*interest in something, one's temper*
make	*a living, a speech*
pass	*a law, sentence (at court)*
pay	*attention, someone a compliment*
read	*between the lines, music*
take	*advantage of someone, offence*

87 Sort out the text 1   *Intermediate*

This is a type of vocabulary cloze activity. The students can work individually or in pairs.

Method

1 Give each pair/groups a copy of the hand-out on page 151.

2 Let them look through it, and then check orally by getting them to take turns at reading sentences out loud.

Key

The parrot and the conjuror
Have you heard about the conjuror who used to entertain the passengers every night on board ship?

Well, every night he gave his show, and every time he did, a parrot used to sit not far away, with his beady eyes fixed on him.

And when the conjuror hid a card up his sleeve, the parrot would croak: "It's up his sleeve!" And when he slipped a rabbit in his pocket, the parrot would croak: "Down his trousers, down his trousers!"

The conjuror was dying to wring his neck.

But one night, when the conjuror was in the middle of his tricks, the ship hit an iceberg, broke in two, and sank almost immediately. The conjuror found himself in the water and thrashed about to keep afloat, until he eventually managed to pull himself up on to an empty raft. He flopped onto it, absolutely exhausted. And who should be perched on the far side of the raft too? The parrot. And the parrot's beady eyes were fixed on the conjuror.

The conjuror just lay there, flat out, for nearly an hour. And all the while the parrot never stirred, and he never for one second took his eyes off the conjuror.

Finally, the conjuror moved, and opened his eyes. And the parrot croaked: "All right, I give up. Where's the ship?"

88 Sort out the text 2 *Intermediate*

This is an example of a jigsaw-reading exercise where a story is completely mixed up. The aim is for the students to put the story in the right order.

Method

1 Put the students in pairs or groups of three. Give each pair/group a copy of the hand-out on page 152.
2 Explain what they have to do. Set a time-limit.
3 Check orally.

Key

Lucky Chris falls from 22 floors up then walks away

A man plunged 200 ft from the top of a tower block yesterday — and walked away almost unhurt. Chris Saggers sailed past twenty two floors of a block of flats before landing on the roof of a parked car.

Seconds later, he climbed out of the wreckage, dusted himself down and walked away. Security guards watching on a video monitor at the council flats in Salford, Greater Manchester, were convinced he was falling to certain death.

They could not believe their eyes when Chris, 26, climbed from the flattened Nissan Micra car and headed off up a side street.

A stunned passer-by rushed to give him the kiss of life, but a very-much-alive Chris muttered: "I'm fine" and walked off.

Police later found him wandering nearby and took him to hospital.

John Whalley, caretaker at the flats said yesterday: "It's an absolute miracle he survived. He must have fallen more than 200 ft and he must have been going at a fair old speed. There was glass everywhere and the car was a complete write-off, but there wasn't a spot of blood anywhere."

Chris, who lives near Salford, was taken to nearby Hope Hospital where his condition last night was described as 'comfortable'. He has a broken elbow, neck injuries and minor cuts and bruises.

The owner of the eight-year-old car, a Salford University student, was planning to sell it. Now he's the owner of a pile of scrap.

89 Sort out the punch lines

Intermediate/Advanced

The final two activities in the book show how jokes and humour can be used in vocabulary learning. The students can work individually or in pairs.

Method

1 Give each student/pair a copy of the hand-out on page 153.
2 Explain what is to be done and check orally. This can be done in dialogue form with the student reading out loud in pairs, but this time putting in the "correct" punch line.

Key

Joke 1 (7) Joke 2 (6) Joke 3 (12) Joke 4 (8)
Joke 5 (1) Joke 6 (9) Joke 7 (10) Joke 8 (4)
Joke 9 (11) Joke 10 (3) Joke 11 (5) Joke 12 (2)

90 Who wrote what? *Advanced*

In this activity, the students have to match up book titles with the correct author. Again, the students can work individually or in pairs.

Method

1 Give each student/pair a copy of the hand-out on page 154.
2 Explain what is to be done and check orally.

Key

Lee King, Lord Howard Hertz, C. Ment,
Walter Wall, Laura Norder, Peter Out,
Claude Legg, Teresa Green, Miss D. Buss,
San Widge, Trudy Light, Liza Lott, Willie Maykit,
Constance Norah, Neil Downe, Sue Nora Later,
U.R.A. Payne, Ellen Back, Anne Teak, B. Keeper

Part 2

Material for photocopying

1 FIND SOMEONE WHO...1

Find someone who: **1**

1 can name three things you would find in a **kitchen**. _____

2 can think of three words that start with **st-**. _____

3 knows what a **loo** is. _____

4 knows what **Stilton, Double Gloucester** and
  Caerphilly are. _____

5 knows where you would find a **cushion**. _____

Find someone who: **2**

1 can name three things you would find in a **bathroom**. _____

2 can think of three words that start with **ex-**. _____

3 knows which animal lives in a **nest**. _____

4 knows what **salmon, pike** and **cod** are. _____

5 knows the opposite of **profit**. _____

Find someone who: **3**

1 can name three things you would find in a **bedroom**. _____

2 can think of three words that start with **cat-**. _____

3 knows what **iron, copper** and **lead** are. _____

4 knows what a **busker** does. _____

5 can think of three words that rhyme with **day**. _____

Find someone who: **4**

1 can name three things that are **sharp**. _____

2 can think of three words that start with **sp-**. _____

3 knows what **thrush, wren** and **hawk** are. _____

4 knows what a **spoke** is part of. _____

5 can think of three words that rhyme with **now**. _____

Find someone who: **5**

1 can name three games you can **play**. _____

2 can think of three words that start with **tr-**. _____

3 knows what **beech, willow** and **spruce** are. _____

4 knows what a **rung** is part of. _____

5 can think of three words that rhyme with **clown**. _____

Find someone who: **6**

1 can name three things that are **fragile**.   _____
2 can think of three words that start with **in-**. _____
3 knows what **ladybird**, **cockroach** and **flea** are. _____
4 knows where you would find a **clutch**.   _____
5 can think of three words that rhyme with **spoon**. _____

Find someone who: **7**

1 can name three things that an **artist** would use. _____
2 can think of three words that start with **re-**. _____
3 knows what **bassoon**, **cello** and **harmonica** are. _____
4 knows where you would find a **mattress**.   _____
5 can think of three words that rhyme with **hole**. _____

Find someone who: **8**

1 can name three things that a **carpenter** would use. _____
2 can think of three words that start with **par-**. _____
3 knows what **snake**, **crocodile** and **lizard** are. _____
4 knows where you would find a **gutter**.   _____
5 can think of three words that rhyme with **love**. _____

Find someone who: **9**

1 can name three things that a **nurse** would use. _____
2 can think of three words that start with **com-**. _____
3 knows what **turnip**, **leek** and **swede** are. _____
4 knows where you would find a **lapel**.   _____
5 knows what a **taxidermist** does.   _____

Find someone who: **10**

1 can name three things that an **electrician** would use. _____
2 can think of three words that start with **de-**. _____
3 knows what **parsley**, **sage** and **thyme** are. _____
4 knows where you would find a **cuff**.   _____
5 knows what you would normally buy in a **punnet**. _____

Find someone who: **11**

1 can name three things that a **teacher** would use.   _____

2 knows two other words for **strange**.   _____

3 knows what the Scottish word **loch** is.   _____

4 knows who would wear a **dog-collar**.   _____

5 knows what you would carry in a **hod**.   _____

Find someone who: **12**

1 can name three things you would wear on your **feet**. _____

2 knows two other words for **very big**.   _____

3 knows what a **brolly** is.   _____

4 knows what the abbreviation **DIY** stands for.   _____

5 knows the American word for **lift**.   _____

Find someone who: **13**

1 can name three things you would wear on your **head**. _____

2 knows two other words for **wonderful**.   _____

3 knows what a **quid** is.   _____

4 knows what the abbreviation **EC** stands for.   _____

5 knows the American word for **tap** (noun).   _____

Find someone who: **14**

1 can name three items of **underwear**.   _____

2 knows two other words for **awful**.   _____

3 knows in which language the word **mochyn**
   means "pig".   _____

4 knows what the abbreviation **BBC** stands for.   _____

5 knows the American word for **holiday**.   _____

Find someone who: **15**

1 can name three **pets** you would keep in a cage.   _____

2 knows two other words for **to hate**.   _____

3 knows where you would find a **saucepan**.   _____

4 knows what the abbreviation **TUC** stands for.   _____

5 knows the American word for **autumn**.   _____

Note to teacher for Card 14: *mochyn* is the Welsh word for pig.

Find someone who: **16**

1 can name three **musical instruments** that you blow. _____
2 knows two other words for **mad**. _____
3 knows where you would find a **deck**, a **funnel** and an **anchor**. _____
4 knows what the abbreviation **VIP** stands for. _____
5 knows the American word for **nappy**. _____

Find someone who: **17**

1 can name three things that are **dangerous**. _____
2 can think of three ways of **walking**. _____
3 knows what **bungalow**, **flat** and **mansion** are. _____
4 knows where you would find a **vest**. _____
5 knows what is sold at a **stationer's**. _____

Find someone who: **18**

1 can name three things you would find in an **office**. _____
2 can think of three ways of **looking**. _____
3 knows where you would find a **platform**, a **waiting room** and a **buffet**. _____
4 knows the opposite of **voluntary**. _____
5 knows when you might use the phrase **Say cheese!** _____

Find someone who: **19**

1 can name three people who wear **uniforms**. _____
2 can think of three ways of **talking**. _____
3 knows what you would use a **grater** for. _____
4 knows the opposite of **entrance**. _____
5 can say when you might use the phrase **Many happy returns!** _____

Find someone who: **20**

1 can name three parts of a **car**. _____
2 can think of three **illnesses** or **diseases**. _____
3 knows where you would find a **parting**. _____
4 knows the opposite of **generous**. _____
5 can say when you might use the phrase **Not at all!** _____

2 FIND SOMEONE WHO...2

Find someone who:

1 can name two fruits that begin with **p**.

_____

2 can name two vegetables that begin with **c**.

_____

3 knows the opposite of
rich
deep
heavy

_____

4 knows how many there are in a **dozen**.

_____

5 knows what you would buy at
a florist's
an ironmonger's

_____

6 knows how many eyes you close when you **wink**.

_____

7 knows who would use
a briefcase
a whistle

_____

8 knows what animal lives in
a kennel
a nest

_____

9 can think of three words that rhyme with **buy**.

_____

10 can name two things found in the
kitchen
bathroom
bedroom

_____

11 knows what you would keep in a **wardrobe**.

_____

12 can name five things you can **drink**.

_____

13 can name five things you can **eat**.

_____

14 knows a synonym for
unhappy   s____
start   b____
depart   l____

_____

15 can name four **wild animals**.

_____

16 can name four **insects**.

_____

17 can name three things worn by
men
women

_____

18 can say which sport uses a **racket**.

_____

19 can name five verbs that begin with **t**.

_____

20 can name five adjectives that begin with **s**.

3 FIND SOMEONE WHO...3

Find someone who:

1 knows which British outdoor game uses **wickets**.

_____

2 knows what a **graphologist** studies.

_____

3 knows four synonyms for **awful**.

_____

4 knows where you would wear a **garter**.

_____

5 knows what someone suffering from **agoraphobia** is afraid of.

_____

6 can rearrange the letters in each of the following words to make three new words.
bleat
toga
resist

_____

7 can think of five words that start with **tri**-.

_____

8 can give one word for each of the following definitions:
loss of memory
a____
a feeling or inclination to vomit
n____
unable to read or write
i____

_____

9 can give a one-syllabled synonym for
serene
endeavour
imbibe

10 can explain the expression **to call a spade a spade**.

_____

11 can give four synonyms for the verb **to hate**.

_____

12 can think of five words that start with **par**-.

_____

13 knows who would use a **baton**.

_____

14 can explain the difference between **recipe** and **receipt**.

_____

15 can name four **natural disasters**.

_____

16 knows what a **blackleg** is.

_____

17 knows five words to do with a **computer**.

_____

18 can explain the phrase **Hobson's choice**.

_____

19 can think of five words that rhyme with **food**.

_____

20 knows the female of
fox
stallion
bull

I'm going to the zoo…	…to see the wild animals.
Let's go to the travel agent…	…to book our summer holiday.
I need some soap…	…to wash my hands.
You'll need a saucepan…	…to boil those potatoes.
You'd better take a torch…	…to see in the dark.
I need a ruler…	…to draw straight lines.
I must go to the optician's…	…to get a new pair of glasses.
You need a passport…	…to travel abroad.
Let's take the lift…	…to get to the top floor.
You can use a dictionary…	…to find out what the word means.

I bought a new sink unit…	…for the kitchen.
He often wears a carnation…	…in his buttonhole.
Have some swede…	…with your dinner.
We went on a cruise…	…last summer.
She got my telephone number…	…from Directory Enquiries.
Put all your luggage…	…in the boot.
She was over £1,000…	…in debt.
We need to buy some disks…	…for our computer.
I try to get a good suntan…	…every summer.
My son wants a pet hamster…	…for his birthday.

Too many cooks…	…spoil the broth.
A stitch in time…	…saves nine.
Absence…	…makes the heart grow fonder.
Still waters…	…run deep.
Actions…	…speak louder than words.
Practice…	…makes perfect.
Charity…	…begins at home.
One good turn…	…deserves another.
A new broom…	…sweeps clean.
Beauty…	…is only skin deep.

I won't get...	...married until I'm...	...at least 25.
I'd change my...	...name if I weren't...	...happy with it.
I won't be able to...	...arrive before...	...Friday, I'm afraid.
I'd get a...	...dog, only my son...	...is afraid of them.
I'm afraid she won't...	...do it unless she...	...gets £500.
I'd ask you to...	...stay, only we don't...	...have a spare room.
He won't be able...	...to play on Saturday...	...owing to injury.
I won't ask...	...David to do it because...	...he's too busy.

8 WORD SETS 1

BABY	cot	dummy	pram
CAR	boot	clutch	tyre
CAT	paw	purr	whiskers
FACE	freckles	eyebrow	temple
HOSPITAL	surgeon	ward	patient

9 WORD SETS 2

WEATHER	storm	hail	forecast
TREE	trunk	twig	bark
BOOK	jacket	index	blurb
FLOWER	petal	stem	daffodil
ATHLETICS	shot	hurdles	relay

10 PICTURE BINGO (teacher's board)

1	2	3	4	5
ASHTRAY	BED	BOOKCASE	CHAIR	CLOCK
6	7	8	9	10
COOKER	CUP	CUPBOARD	GLASS	HAMMER
11	12	13	14	15
KNIFE	LAMP	PLATE	SCISSORS	SPOON
16	17	18	19	20
TABLE	TELEPHONE	TELEVISION	UMBRELLA	VASE

11 OPPOSITES BINGO (teacher's board)

1	2	3	4	5
BEAUTIFUL (ugly)	BIG (small)	CLEAN (dirty)	DEAD (alive)	DRY (wet)
6	7	8	9	10
EASY (difficult)	EXPENSIVE (cheap)	HAPPY (sad)	HARD (soft)	HOT (cold)
11	12	13	14	15
LATE (early)	LIGHT (heavy)	LOW (high)	OLD (young)	RICH (poor)
16	17	18	19	20
RIGHT (wrong)	SLOW (quick)	TALL (short)	THICK (thin)	WEAK (strong)

12 PREPOSITIONS BINGO (teacher's board)

1 about	2 above	3 across	4 after	5 against	6 at
7 between	8 by	9 down	10 for	11 from	12 in
13 into	14 next to	15 of	16 on	17 outside	18 over
19 round	20 since	21 through	22 to	23 under	24 with

13 SYNONYMS BINGO (teacher's board)

1 AWFUL (terrible)	2 CAUTIOUS (careful)	3 DIZZY (giddy)	4 EAGER (keen)	5 ENORMOUS (huge)
6 EXPENSIVE (dear)	7 FRIGHTENED (scared)	8 GOOD-LOOKING (handsome)	9 HAPPY (glad)	10 HOPEFUL (optimistic)
11 IMPOLITE (rude)	12 MAD (insane)	13 OBSTINATE (stubborn)	14 PECULIAR (strange)	15 PLEASANT (nice)
16 SAD (unhappy)	17 RICH (wealthy)	18 POLITE (well-mannered)	19 WICKED (evil)	20 WONDERFUL (marvellous)

14 DEFINITIONS BINGO (teacher's board)

1	2	3	4	5
all the actors in a play or film (CAST)	a written account of someone's life (BIOGRAPHY)	the place where bread is made (BAKERY)	the skin of an orange, an apple, etc. (PEEL)	a period of ten years (DECADE)
6	**7**	**8**	**9**	**10**
a very strong wind (GALE)	the meat we get from a calf (VEAL)	the place where dead people are buried (CEMETERY)	a small stream (BROOK)	the main part of a tree (TRUNK)
11	**12**	**13**	**14**	**15**
a common yellow spring flower (DAFFODIL)	the middle part of an apple (CORE)	the place in a car where you put luggage (BOOT)	the person in charge of a museum (CURATOR)	a tool used by a carpenter (PLANE)
16	**17**	**18**	**19**	**20**
a room where an artist or photographer works (STUDIO)	someone who regularly travels a long distance to work (COMMUTER)	the place where a town's water supply is stored (RESERVOIR)	goods for sale (STOCK)	a place where fish are kept indoors (AQUARIUM)

15 PARTS OF THE BODY IDIOMS BINGO (teacher's board)

1	2	3	4	5
back	**blood**	**brain**	**ears**	**eye**
6	**7**	**8**	**9**	**10**
face	**fingers**	**flesh**	**feet**	**hair**
11	**12**	**13**	**14**	**15**
hand	**head**	**heart**	**heels**	**leg**
16	**17**	**18**	**19**	**20**
lip	**mind**	**mouth**	**neck**	**nose**
21	**22**	**23**	**24**	**25**
shoulder	**skin**	**throat**	**tongue**	**tooth**

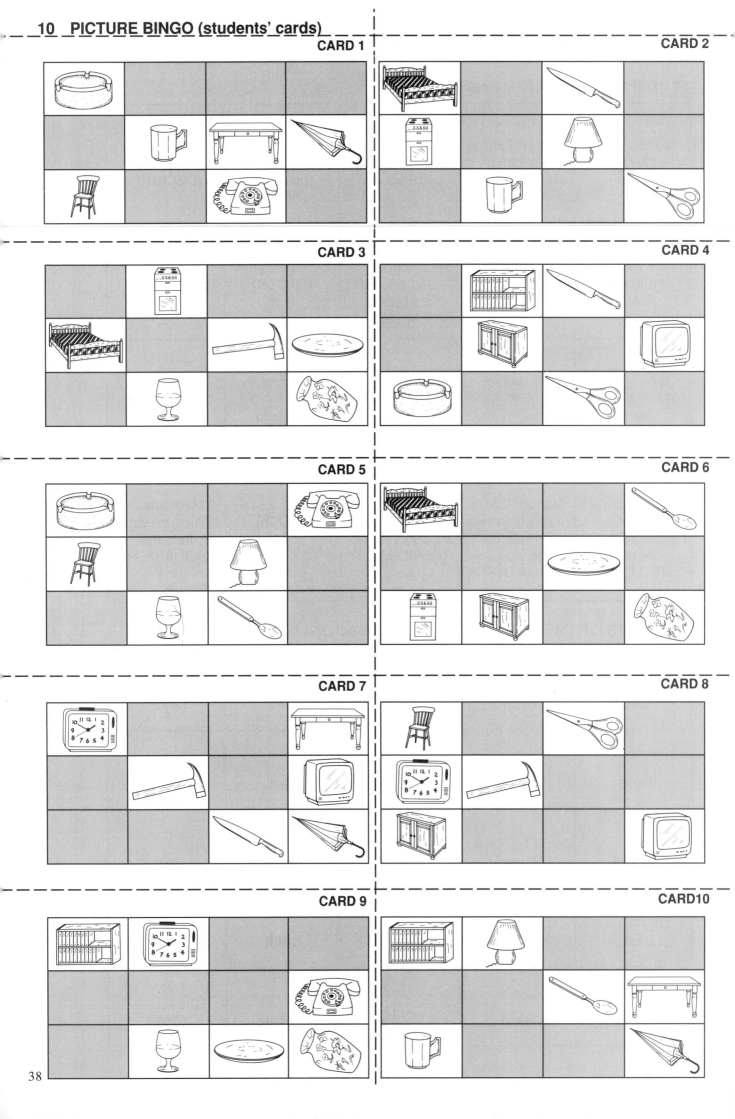

11 OPPOSITES BINGO (students' cards)

CARD 1

alive			
	early	thin	wrong
cheap		ugly	

CARD 2

alive		small	
heavy		wet	
	quick		young

CARD 3

	cold		
cheap		small	soft
	high		strong

CARD 4

	early	short	
	sad		young
dirty		ugly	

CARD 5

heavy			wet
poor		soft	
	quick	ugly	

CARD 6

cheap			small
		sad	
high	poor		strong

CARD 7

cold			short
	difficult		thin
		early	wrong

CARD 8

cold		wet	
difficult	short		
sad			young

CARD 9

difficult	dirty		
			soft
	high	quick	strong

CARD 10

alive	heavy		
		poor	thin
dirty			wrong

39

12   PREPOSITIONS BINGO (students' cards)

CARD 1

1 He gave me a book _____ fishing.
2 He went out of the room to do something, but returned _____ a few minutes.
3 Share this bar of chocolate _____ you and David.
4 My husband comes _____ Sweden.
5 The post office is _____ the library.

CARD 2

1 The people in the flat _____ mine were having a party last night.
2 The bus driver was leaning _____ the side of the bus.
3 I usually go to work _____ bus.
4 Tears ran _____ her cheek as she watched the film.
5 I bought three pints _____ milk.

CARD 3

1 Today was the first time the temperature had risen _____ zero.
2 Stop leaning _____ my car!
3 The quickest way of travelling is _____ air.
4 We start work again _____ Monday.
5 She put her arms _____ me and gave me a kiss.

CARD 4

1 He dared me to jump _____ the stream.
2 There's a car park _____ the cinema and the supermarket.
3 Put these flowers _____ the vase.
4 He wore a pullover _____ his shirt.
5 You go on. You don't have to wait _____ me.

CARD 5

1 We went _____ the road to the post office.
2 I think I'll stay _____ home tonight.
3 My sister has been living in Brighton _____ ten years.
4 He is very fond _____ children.
5 Would you like a sandwich _____ your coffee?

CARD 6

1 She arrived home just _____ midnight – two minutes past to be exact.
2 I usually go out _____ the weekend.
3 It's three months since I heard _____ Jennifer.
4 You can sit down _____ my grandfather.
5 Are there any good programmes _____ television tonight?

CARD 7

1 Go _____ this street as far as the car park, then turn right.
2 My father is very interested _____ football.
3 We stood _____ the shop waiting for it to open.
4 We haven't seen Cathy _____ 1992.
5 We couldn't see the cat at first because he was asleep _____ the bed.

CARD 8

1 He got _____ bed and was soon fast asleep.
2 I'll meet you _____ the entrance to the hotel at 7.30.
3 She hung some flowers _____ my neck.
4 The rain came in _____ a hole in the roof.
5 He was in love _____ his teacher.

CARD 9

1 The film was _____ a man looking for his daughter.
2 She knocked before she walked _____ the room.
3 They are going to build a bridge _____ the river here.
4 We took a short cut home _____ the park.
5 Shall we go _____ the cinema tonight?

CARD 10

1 I've been living _____ France for three years.
2 He had a big party _____ his birthday.
3 I haven't smoked _____ last June.
4 Are you looking forward _____ the summer?
5 We keep a wastepaper bin _____ the sink.

13 SYNONYMS BINGO (students' cards)

CARD 1

dear			
	rude	scared	unhappy
evil		terrible	

CARD 2

careful		scared	
insane		strange	
	keen		wealthy

CARD 3

	dear		
careful		marvellous	optimistic
	glad		stubborn

CARD 4

	handsome	strange	
	rude		well-mannered
giddy		terrible	

CARD 5

glad			wealthy
insane		nice	
	keen	terrible	

CARD 6

careful			nice
		marvellous	
dear	handsome		stubborn

CARD 7

evil			rude
	huge		unhappy
		optimistic	well-mannered

CARD 8

handsome		strange	
huge	optimistic		
keen			well-mannered

CARD 9

giddy	glad		
			stubborn
	huge	marvellous	wealthy

CARD 10

evil	insane		
		nice	scared
giddy			unhappy

41

CARD 1

aquarium			
	cemetery	daffodil	studio
cast		plane	

CARD 2

bakery		decade	
biography		reservoir	
	cemetery		veal

CARD 3

	cast		
biography		curator	gale
	core		trunk

CARD 4

	boot	daffodil	
	commuter		veal
aquarium		stock	

CARD 5

aquarium			reservoir
bakery		decade	
	core	peel	

CARD 6

biography			peel
		gale	
cast	commuter		trunk

CARD 7

brook			plane
	curator		stock
		daffodil	studio

CARD 8

bakery		stock	
brook	curator		
commuter			veal

CARD 9

boot	brook		
			reservoir
	core	gale	trunk

CARD 10

boot	decade		
		peel	plane
cemetery			studio

42

15 PARTS OF THE BODY IDIOMS BINGO (students' cards)

CARD 1

1 To do something behind someone's _____. (= act deceitfully)

2 To keep a straight _____. (= not to laugh)

3 To escape by a _____'s breadth. (= only just escape)

4 To show a clean pair of _____. (= run away quickly)

5 To be down in the _____. (= be unhappy)

CARD 2

1 To have one's _____ to the wall. (= struggle against difficulties)

2 To be all _____ and thumbs. (= be clumsy)

3 To set one's _____ on something. (= want something very much)

4 To be up to one's _____ in debt. (= be deeply in debt)

5 To make one's _____ boil. (= make one very angry)

CARD 3

1 To have something on the _____. (= be obsessive about something)

2 To see someone in the _____. (= actually see someone)

3 To have a big _____. (= be generous)

4 None of your _____! (= Don't speak to me like that!)

5 To be as plain as the _____ on your face. (= be obvious)

CARD 4

1 A _____wave. (= a sudden, clever idea)

2 To stand on one's own two _____. (= be independent)

3 To bite a person's _____ off. (= speak angrily to someone)

4 To jump out of one's _____. (= be startled)

5 To have a sweet _____. (= like eating sweet things)

CARD 5

1 To be wet behind the _____. (= be young and inexperienced)

2 To try one's _____ at something. (= try to do something new)

3 To pull someone's _____. (= tease someone)

4 To be all _____ and bone. (= very thin)

5 One's own flesh and _____. (= one's own family)

CARD 6

1 To be all _____. (= listen very carefully)

2 To make one's _____ creep. (= be terrified)

3 To be head over _____ in love. (= be completely in love)

4 To go out of one's _____. (= go mad)

5 To have a chip on one's _____. (= have a grievance)

CARD 7

1 To catch someone's _____. (= attract someone's attention)

2 To have green _____. (= be good at gardening)

3 To go off one's _____. (= go mad)

4 To make up one's _____. (= decide)

5 To be a pain in the _____. (= be a pest and a nuisance)

CARD 8

1 To pay through the _____. (= pay too much)

2 To have a _____ as long as a fiddle. (= look depressed)

3 To show a _____. (= get out of bed)

4 To keep a stiff upper _____. (= bear trouble without showing emotion)

5 To keep one's _____ on. (= stay calm, not become angry)

CARD 9

1 To get cold _____. (= be afraid, lose courage)

2 To be long in the _____. (= be old)

3 To give someone the cold _____. (=ignore someone)

4 To jump down someone's _____. (= speak angrily to someone)

5 To hold one's _____. (= remain silent)

CARD 10

1 To give someone a _____ with something. (= help someone)

2 To look as if butter wouldn't melt in one's _____. (= look very innocent)

3 To turn a blind _____ to something. (= deliberately ignore something)

4 To have a lump in one's _____. (= feel sad, be about to cry)

5 To lose one's _____. (= be too shy to speak)

answer	**ask**
blow	**brush**
build	**climb**
cook	**catch**
draw	**drink**
drive	**eat**
fasten	**play**
read	**ride**
sing	**smoke**
switch on	**write**

the phone	*a question*
your nose	*your teeth*
a house	*a mountain*
a meal	*a cold*
a picture	*a cup of tea*
a car	*a biscuit*
a seatbelt	*the guitar*
a magazine	*a horse*
a song	*a cigar*
the television	*a postcard*

How are you?	Thanks for the lovely party.
Do you mind if I smoke?	I'm sorry I'm late.
I hope England wins the World Cup.	I've just got married.
Help yourself to a drink.	Have a nice weekend.
Would you help me with this, please?	Have you got a light, please?
Did you have a good trip?	Hello. May I join you?
I can't come tonight, I'm afraid.	Could you give me a lift home tonight?
Today's the 4th, isn't it?	Thank you very much.
Another drink, Paul?	Is it far to the station?
Shall I help you with that?	It's a lovely day today, isn't it?

Very well, thank you.	*It's a pleasure. I'm glad you liked it.*
No, of course not.	*Oh, that's all right.*
So do I.	*Congratulations!*
Thank you.	*Thanks. The same to you.*
Yes, certainly.	*Sorry, I don't smoke.*
Yes, not too bad, thanks.	*Yes, please do.*
Oh, what a pity!	*Yes, I'd be glad to.*
Yes, that's right.	*You're welcome!*
No, not just now, thanks.	*No, not very.*
No, there's no need, thanks.	*Yes, beautiful.*

crash helmet	**whistle**
word processor	**palette**
pins	**(black)board**
saw	**comb**
hose	**stethoscope**
rifle	**till**
spanner	**handcuffs**
sleeping bag	**screwdriver**
wheelbarrow	**baton**
tractor	**briefcase**

motorcyclist	*referee*
secretary	*artist*
dressmaker	*teacher*
carpenter	*barber*
fireman	*doctor*
soldier	*shop assistant*
mechanic	*policeman*
camper	*electrician*
gardener	*conductor*
farmer	*businessman*

annual	blunt
courteous	damp
deliberate	drowsy
durable	fragile
fragrant	furious
huge	illegible
illiterate	invisible
peckish	placid
reluctant	rude
snug	urgent

happening once a year	*not sharp (e.g. a knife)*
polite, well-mannered	*rather wet*
something that is done on purpose	*sleepy*
strong and long-lasting	*delicate; easily damaged*
sweet-smelling	*very angry; raging*
extremely large	*difficult or impossible to read*
unable to read or write	*that cannot be seen*
slightly hungry	*calm; not easily upset*
unwilling, hesitant	*bad-mannered, impolite*
warm and cosy	*so important that it needs to be dealt with at once*

an anthology of	an article of
an attack of	a beam of
a blade of	a board of
a breath of	a bunch of
a clap of	a collection of
a flash of	a fit of
a flock of	a herd of
an item of	a joint of
a pane of	a plot of
a rasher of	a stroke of

poems	clothing
nerves	light
grass	directors
fresh air	keys
thunder	short stories
lightning	anger
sheep	cows
news	meat
glass	land
bacon	luck

break	**bring**
fall	**get**
give	**go**
have	**hold**
keep	**make**
pull	**put**
take	**bark**
burn	**feather**
hit	**let**
talk	**wet**

the ice	the house down
over oneself to do something	into hot water
someone the slip	for a song
a flutter	one's tongue
something under one's hat	both ends meet
one's socks up	one's foot down
the bull by the horns	up the wrong tree
the midnight oil	one's nest
the nail on the head	the cat out of the bag
through the top of one's hat	one's whistle

viewfinder (n)	loft (adj)
apparent (n)	megahertz (n pl)
awl (n)	microwave (n)
defeated (adj)	otter (adj)
destabilize (v)	paperweight (n)
exile (n)	perspire (adv)
Hebrew (n)	Polynesia (n)
impeccable (adj)	psychic (n)
intense (n pl)	snorkel (n)
limbo (n)	universe (n)

a tour guide	mifplafed or perhapf ftolen
a large, old, bossy person whose only function is to torture young people	one million aches and pains
gold, to a Texan	a form of greeting popular with computer programmers
chopped off at the ankles	a Cockney weather forecast
to take the horse out for a trot	a bureaucratic delay
a former island	the way church builders calculate their construction costs
a macho glass of beer	loss of memory in parrots
unable to be eaten by a chicken	a faithful companion
where nomads and happy campers sleep	a cross between a snore and a chuckle
the place where arms and legs go when they die	an all-purpose poem

BOARD FOR DOMINOES

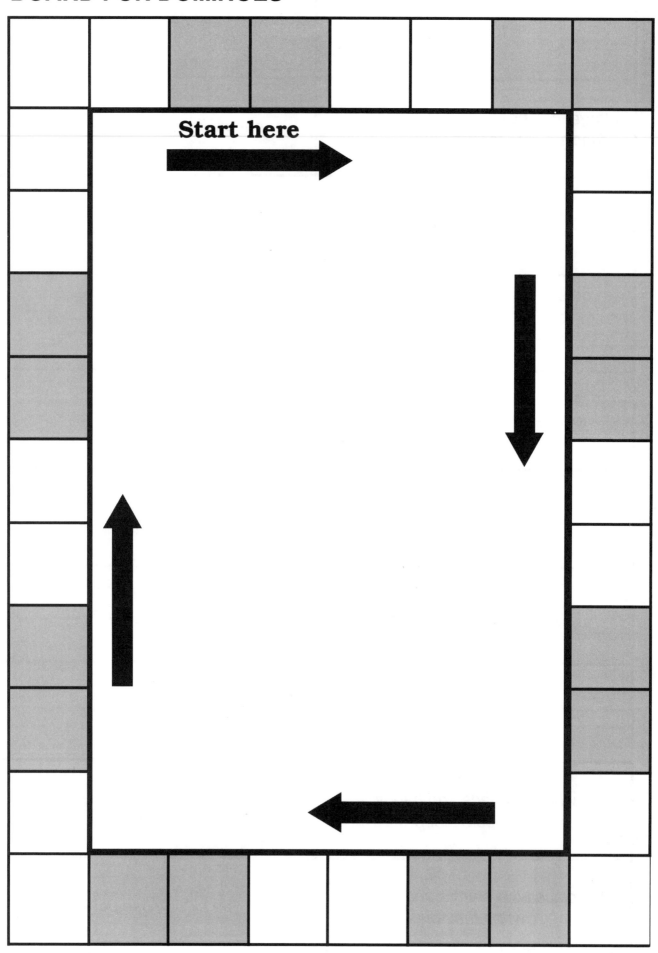

Start here

23 DOMINOES: NOUNS 1

box	bath	room	coffee	table	chest	nut	sauce
pan	vacuum	cleaner	book	case	fire	work	light
bulb	dish	washer	tea	spoon	arm	chair	pen
knife	coat	hanger	sun	glasses	drain	pipe	seat
belt	letter						

24 DOMINOES: NOUNS 2

ground	car	pet	lady	bird	board	room	test
tube	sky	light	ice	cream	cross	word	motor
way	butter	fly	wind	screen	dust	pan	ear
wig	post	card	shoe	lace	suit	case	phrase
book	under						

25 DOMINOES: NOUNS 3

bar	rain	fall	dip	stick	chin	wag	head
strong	cast	away	lay	man	bar	gain	paper
back	man	hole	cow	slip	had	dock	over
sight	back	log	busy	body	under	dog	fire
arm	cross						

26 DOMINOES: CLOTHES

sers	co	at	glo	ves	su	it	jac
ket	sh	irt	blo	use	dr	ess	je
ans	sh	oes	so	cks	sc	arf	ve
st	ski	rt	pyj	amas	jum	per	be
lt	trou						

27 DOMINOES: PHRASAL VERBS

match, suit	*fall out*	quarrel	*look into*	investi-gate	*pass out*	faint	*do up*
decorate, modernize	*call off*	cancel	*go out (fire)*	stop burning	*pass away*	die	*turn down*
refuse	*blow up*	explode	*look up to*	admire, respect	*get over*	recover from	*call on*
visit	*own up*	confess	*drop off*	fall asleep	*put off*	postpone	*give in*
yield, surrender	*go with*						

28 DOMINOES: IDIOMS

very frightening	*nosy*	inquisitive, curious	*down-at-heel*	shabbily dressed	*hard up*	poor, short of money	*big-headed*
vain, conceited	*cheesed off*	fed up, bored	*off one's head*	mad, insane	*all thumbs*	very clumsy	*dead beat*
completely exhausted	*keyed up*	tense, excited	*down-to-earth*	sensible, practical	*on the dole*	unemployed	*long in the tooth*
old	*pig-headed*	stubborn	*off colour*	ill, not well	*tight-fisted*	mean, miserly	*thick-skinned*
insensitive, not easily offended	*hair-raising*						

birds	birthday	book	briefcase
cake	car	cat	choose
cinema	clothes	doctor	family
fat	film	fish and chips	food
football	fruit	garden	ghost
happy	holiday	hospital	house
hungry	ill	jacket	job
keep fit	library	milk	money
mosquito	motorway	nervous	old
Paris	party	photograph	policeman
present	purple	quarrel	rain
restaurant	run	school	spider
sport	student	summer	waiter

accident	accountant	Austria	avalanche
bicycle	big-headed	burglary	Christmas
cigarette	cinema	compulsory	dinner party
divorce	dustbin	frightened	generous
hijack	hitchhike	hungry	ice cream
in love	jealous	kiss	kitten
make a speech	measles	moustache	overcoat
plumber	pregnant	prejudiced	prescription
ring	river	roses	sister
skirt	snake	sports car	station
strawberries	stubborn	suntan	thirsty
tie	toothache	trade union	traffic warden
turkey	village	wealthy	wedding

advertisement	ambitious	astrology	bald
bargain	boring	charity	cheeky
conference	control	cruise	depressed
disappointed	down in the mouth	drugs	earthquake
Eiffel Tower	elephant	envious	estate agent
feel sorry for	fiancé	get the sack	gypsies
headline	hilarious	housework	illegal
insomnia	lonely	Look out!	nuclear power station
overtake	overweight	peckish	postpone
president	receipt	refugee	rubber plant
shipwrecked	shoplifting	shy	spaghetti
steal	strike	superstitious	surgeon
Switzerland	unemployed	weekend	wig

32 HALF A CROSSWORD: SPORTS, HOBBIES AND PASTIMES

Work in Groups A and B. You are A.

The crossword below is only half filled in. Group B also have a crossword that is only half filled in. Take it in turns to ask what the missing words are (e.g. "What's 3 across?") and answer by trying to explain each word.

Here are the words you will have to explain to Group B:

athletics	dancing	gymnastics	knitting	rugby
chess	darts	judo	pottery	snooker

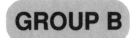

Work in Groups A and B. You are B.

The crossword below is only half filled in. Group A also have a crossword that is only half filled in. Take it in turns to ask what the missing words are (e.g. "What's 2 down?") and answer by trying to explain each word.

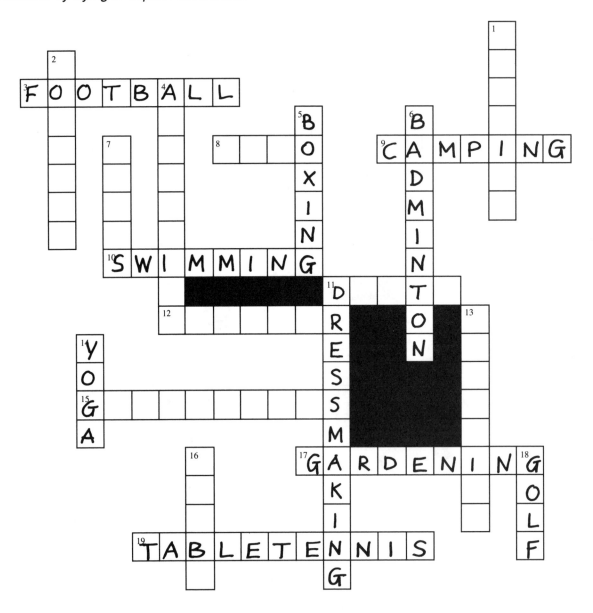

Here are the words you will have to explain to Group A:

badminton	camping	football	golf	table tennis
boxing	dressmaking	gardening	swimming	yoga

© Penguin Books Ltd 1993

33 HALF A CROSSWORD: JOBS AND OCCUPATIONS

Work in Groups A and B. You are A.

The crossword below is only half filled in. Group B also have a crossword that is only half filled in. Take it in turns to ask what the missing words are (e.g. "What's 3 across?") and answer by trying to explain each word.

Here are the words you will have to explain to Group B:

actor	carpenter	dentist	hairdresser	vet
baker	chef	doctor	librarian	waiter
butcher				

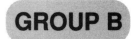
Work in Groups A and B. You are B.

The crossword below is only half filled in. Group A also have a crossword that is only half filled in. Take it in turns to ask what the missing words are (e.g. "What's 1 down?") and answer by trying to explain each word..

Here are the words you will have to explain to Group A:

architect	farmer	miner	pilot	secretary
barber	journalist	nurse	salesman	traffic warden
dustman				

© Penguin Books Ltd 1993

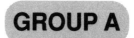

Work in Groups A and B. You are A.

The crossword below is only half filled in. Group B also have a crossword that is only half filled in. Take it in turns to ask what the missing words are (e.g. "What's 9 across?") and answer by trying to explain each word.

Here are the nouns you will have to explain to Group B:

avalanche	choir	niece	stream
beard	comb	pet	suburb
burglary	cream	plant	view
cash	essay	snake	wedding

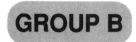

GROUP B

Work in Groups A and B. You are B.

The crossword below is only half filled in. Group A also have a crossword that is only half filled in. Take it in turns to ask what the missing words are (e.g. "What's 1 down?") and answer by trying to explain each word..

Here are the nouns you will have to explain to Group A:

advertisement	bucket	eyelash	nephew
attic	cage	funeral	poem
bar	computer	guitar	suntan
bargain	election	invention	thunder

35 HALF A CROSSWORD: VERBS

Work in Groups A and B. You are A.

The crossword below is only half filled in. Group B also have a crossword that is only half filled in. Take it in turns to ask what the missing words are (e.g. "What's 2 across?") and answer by trying to explain each word.

Here are the verbs you will have to explain to Group B:

admire	exaggerate	nag	refuse
bribe	force	obey	satisfy
deny	hesitate	pollute	sneeze
encourage	invent	quote	survive
envy			

© Penguin Books Ltd 1993

71

Work in Groups A and B. You are B.

The crossword below is only half filled in. Group A also have a crossword that is only half filled in. Take it in turns to ask what the missing words are (e.g. "What's 1 down?") and answer by trying to explain each word..

Here are the verbs you will have to explain to Group A:

abolish	dare	gossip	recognize
afford	discover	oversleep	replace
annoy	estimate	overtake	suspect
boast	execute	play truant	tow
cure			

© Penguin Books Ltd 1993

36 HALF A CROSSWORD: ADJECTIVES TO DESCRIBE PEOPLE

Work in Groups A and B. You are A.

The crossword below is only half filled in. Group B also have a crossword that is only half filled in. Take it in turns to ask what the missing words are (e.g. "What's 3 across?") and answer by trying to explain each word.

Here are the adjectives you will have to explain to Group B:

bossy	handsome	lazy	polite	selfish
cruel	irresponsible	mean	punctual	sensitive
friendly	jealous	modest	reliable	witty

73

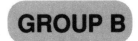
Work in Groups A and B. You are B.

The crossword below is only half filled in. Group A also have a crossword that is only half filled in. Take it in turns to ask what the missing words are (e.g. "What's 1 down?") and answer by trying to explain each word..

Here are the adjectives you will have to explain to Group A:

affectionate	generous	moody	rude	spoilt
brave	honest	patient	sensible	stubborn
cheerful	imaginative	prejudiced	sociable	sympathetic

© Penguin Books Ltd 1993

37 HALF A CROSSWORD: TYPES OF PEOPLE

Work in Groups A and B. You are A.

The crossword below is only half filled in. Group B also have a crossword that is only half filled in. Take it in turns to ask what the missing words are (e.g. "What's 3 across?") and answer by trying to explain each word

Here are the words you will have to explain to Group B:

accomplice	client	genius	midwife	predecessor
acquaintance	deserter	heir	opponent	tourist
chatterbox	gangster	hooligan	partner	

37 HALF A CROSSWORD: TYPES OF PEOPLE

Work in Groups A and B. You are B.

The crossword below is only half filled in. Group A also have a crossword that is only half filled in. Take it in turns to ask what the missing words are (e.g. "What's 1 down?") and answer by trying to explain each word..

Here are the words you will have to explain to Group A:

aristocrat	colleague	orphan	spinster	vegetarian
bachelor	hermit	pedestrian	stowaway	witness
celebrity	neighbour	refugee	successor	

© Penguin Books Ltd 1993

38 SORT OUT THE CLUES

In this crossword, all the words have been filled in. Sort out which clue goes with each word. Write the correct answer (1 down, 8 across, etc.) in front of each clue. Then arrange the clues in two columns, the Across clues in one and the Down clues in the other.

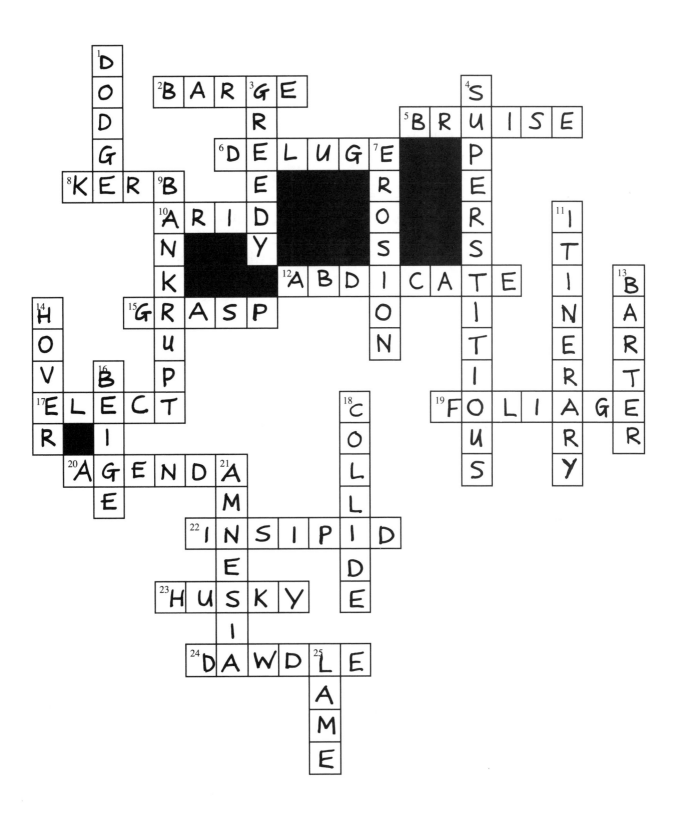

	dry; parched with heat
	unable to pay debts
	a light brown colour
	desiring food, money, etc. in a selfish way
	having a hoarse, whispering voice
	without flavour or strong character
	not able to walk properly
	believing in luck, chance and magic happenings
	to give up a position of power, usually that of a king or queen
	to exchange goods for other goods without using money
	to bump into something by mistake
	to move slowly, to waste time
	to get quickly out of the way
	to choose by voting
	to take firm hold of
	to stay in the air in one place
	a list of things to be dealt with or discussed at a meeting
	loss of memory
	a flat-bottomed boat used on canals and rivers
	a blue-black mark on the skin caused by a knock
	a heavy rainstorm; a downpour
	the slow wearing away of the land by wind, water, etc.
	the leaves of a plant
	a plan or record of a journey
	the stone edge of a pavement

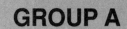
GROUP A

Take it in turns to ask for a letter, e.g. "Is there a letter in 1C?"

If you think you know what the word is you can say: "We think the word from 1A to 1D is _____."
The first group to find all the words wins.

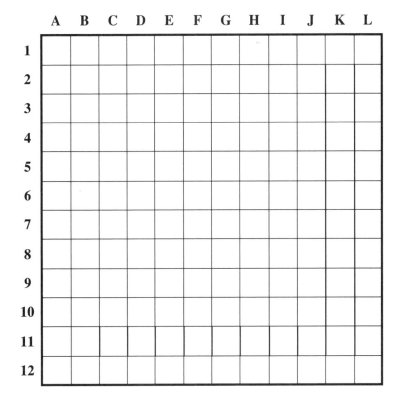

You have to find the following:

two vegetables
two things in the bathroom
two items of clothing
two jobs
two colours

There are:
four words vertically
four words horizontally
two words diagonally

These are the words Group B have to find:

two fruits
pear (2B–2E)
banana (7B–11B)

two things in the kitchen
cooker (5D–10I)
plate (6G–6K)

two animals
cow (1K–3K)
horse (12D–12H)

two numbers
twenty (4L–9L)
eight (6C–10G)

two shops
florist (4E–4K)
butcher (1A–7A)

39 WORD BATTLESHIPS 1

Take it in turns to ask for a letter, e.g. "Is there a letter in 1C?"

If you think you know what the word is you can say: "We think the word from 1A to 1D is _____."
The first group to find all the words wins.

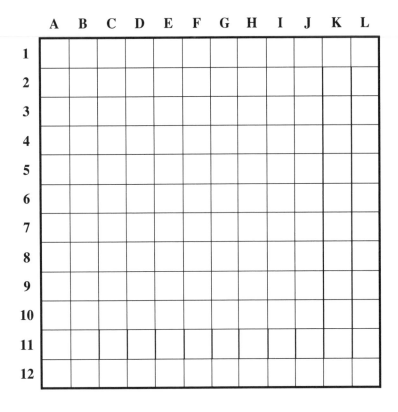

You have to find the following:

two fruits
two things in the kitchen
two animals
two numbers
two shops

There are:
four words vertically
four words horizontally
two words diagonally

These are the words Group A have to find:

two vegetables
carrot (2B–7G)
potato (1G–1L)

two things in the bathroom
toothbrush (3J–12J)
soap (8A–11D)

two items of clothing
skirt (6A–6E)
jumper (2D–2I)

two jobs
waitress (4H–11H)
policeman (12A–12I)

two colours
yellow (4L–9L)
purple (7A–7F)

© Penguin Books Ltd 1993

40 WORD BATTLESHIPS 2

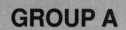

GROUP A

Take it in turns to ask for a letter, e.g. "Is there a letter in 1C?"

If you think you know what the word is you can say: "We think the word from 1A to 1D is _____."
The first group to find all the words wins.

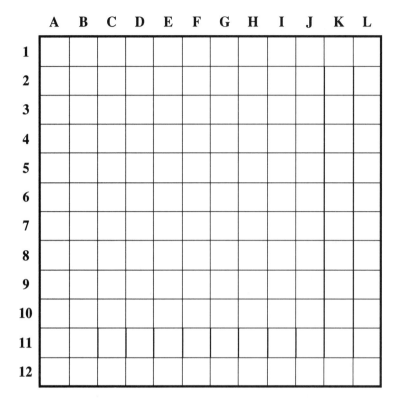

	A	B	C	D	E	F	G	H	I	J	K	L
1												
2												
3												
4												
5												
6												
7												
8												
9												
10												
11												
12												

You have to find the following:

two places to live (homes/dwellings)
two vegetables
two sounds made by people
two synonyms for *very big*
two vehicles

There are:
four words vertically
four words horizontally
two words diagonally

	A	B	C	D	E	F	G	H	I	J	K	L
1	P	T	R	A	I	T	O	R				R
2		E		D	R	E	A	D	F	U	L	A
3			A									S
4				C			P		A			P
5	H				H		E		P			B
6		O					E		P	S		E
7			O				R		A	Q		R
8				L					L	U		R
9					I				L	A		Y
10	W	A	T	E	R		G			I	S	
11							A		N	H		
12	G	L	A	N	C	E		N	G			

These are the words Group B have to find:

two types of people
traitor (1B–1H)
hooligan (5A–12H)

two fruits
raspberry (1L–9L)
peach (1A–5E)

two ways of looking
peer (4G–7G)
glance (12A–12F)

two synonyms for awful
appalling (4I–12I)
dreadful (2D–2K)

two drinks
water (10A–10E)
squash (6J–11J)

Take it in turns to ask for a letter, e.g. "Is there a letter in 1C?"

If you think you know what the word is you can say: "We think the word from 1A to 1D is _____."
The first group to find all the words wins.

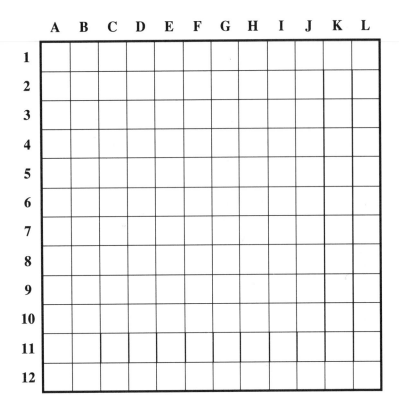

You have to find the following:

two types of people
two fruits
two ways of looking
two synonyms for *awful*
two drinks

There are:
four words vertically
four words horizontally
two words diagonally

These are the words Group A have to find:

two places to live (homes / dwellings)
bungalow (1G–8G)
caravan (12A–12G)

two vegetables
leek (2B–5E)
asparagus (4I–12I)

two sounds made by people
hiccup (5A–10A)
snore (1B–1F)

two synonyms for very big
huge (1I–4L)
enormous (5K–12K)

two vehicles
van (8C–8E)
tram (10C–10F)

The lower grid:

	A	B	C	D	E	F	G	H	I	J	K	L
1		S	N	O	R	E	B		H			
2		L					U			U		
3			E				N				G	
4				E			G		A			E
5	H				K		A		S		E	
6	I						L		P		N	
7	C						O		A		O	
8	C		V	A	N		W		R		R	
9	U								A		M	
10	P		T	R	A	M			G		O	
11									U		U	
12	C	A	R	A	V	A	N		S		S	

© Penguin Books Ltd 1993

41 WORD BATTLESHIPS 3

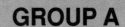

Take it in turns to ask for a letter, e.g. "Is there a letter in 1C?"

If you think you know what the word is you can say: "We think the word from 1A to 1D is _____."
The first group to find all the words wins.

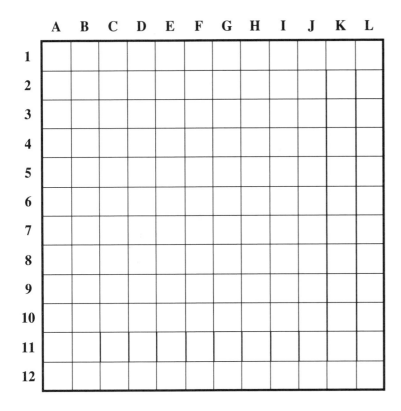

You have to find the following:

two insects
two synonyms for *hate*
two kitchen utensils
two birds
two ways of talking

There are:
four words vertically
four words horizontally
two words diagonally

	A	B	C	D	E	F	G	H	I	J	K	L
1							S					S
2	T	I	E					A				P
3		E	N	G	I	N	E		W			A
4				A								N
5					P							N
6	M	A	R	C	H		R			S		E
7								O		T		R
8	P	E	C	U	L	I	A	R	N	A		B
9										G		R
10				O						G		A
11				D						E		K
12				D						R		E

These are the words Group B have to find:

two items of clothing
tie (2A–2C)
apron (4E–8I)

two synonyms for strange
odd (10D–12D)
peculiar (8A–8H)

two tools
spanner (1L–7L)
saw (1G–3I)

two parts of a car
brake (8L–12L)
engine (3B–3G)

two ways of walking
stagger (6J–12J)
march (6A–6E)

41 WORD BATTLESHIPS 3

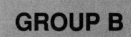

Take it in turns to ask for a letter, e.g. "Is there a letter in 1C?"

If you think you know what the word is you can say: "We think the word from 1A to 1D is _____."
The first group to find all the words wins.

	A	B	C	D	E	F	G	H	I	J	K	L
1												
2												
3												
4												
5												
6												
7												
8												
9												
10												
11												
12												

You have to find the following:

two items of clothing
two synonyms for *strange*
two tools
two parts of a car
two ways of walking

There are:
four words vertically
four words horizontally
two words diagonally

	A	B	C	D	E	F	G	H	I	J	K	L
1	S			D		B		S	P	O	O	N
2	T			E		E						
3	U			T		C		E				
4	T			E		U			T			
5	T	W		S		C	W			L		
6	E	H		T		K		A			E	
7	R	I				O			S			
8		S				O				P		
9		P			S	P	A	R	R	O	W	
10		E										
11		R			S	A	U	C	E	P	A	N
12	L	O	A	T	H	E						

These are the words Group A have to find:

two insects
wasp (5G–8J)
beetle (1F–6K)

two synonyms for hate
loathe (12A–12F)
detest (1D–6D)

two kitchen utensils
saucepan (11E–11L)
spoon (1H–1L)

two birds
cuckoo (3F–8F)
sparrow (9E–9K)

two ways of talking
whisper (5B–11B)
stutter (1A–7A)

84 © Penguin Books Ltd 1993

IN THE KITCHEN	IN THE BATHROOM	IN THE BEDROOM	IN THE LIVING ROOM	IN THE GARDEN
cooker	shampoo	bed	armchair	flowers
fridge	shower	blanket	bookcase	lawn
frying pan	soap	dressing table	coffee table	path
kettle	toothbrush	pillow	sofa	fruit trees
plates	towel	wardrobe	CD player	shed

FISH	BIRDS	KITCHEN UTENSILS	CONTAINERS	TOOLS/ GARDENING EQUIPMENT
cod	crow	frying pan	barrel	axe
herring	owl	grater	basket	hammer
salmon	parrot	rolling pin	cage	lawnmower
trout	pigeon	saucepan	dustbin	screwdriver
tuna	sparrow	toaster	sack	spade

BIG	BRAVE	DARK	SAD	POOR
enormous	bold	dim	dejected	broke
gigantic	courageous	dusky	depressed	destitute
huge	daring	gloomy	downcast	hard up
massive	fearless	obscure	miserable	needy
vast	unafraid	sombre	unhappy	penniless

HIT	LAUGH AND SMILE	STEAL	CRY	CUT
beat	beam	burgle	blubber	chop
flog	giggle	embezzle	snivel	fell
slap	grin	loot	sob	hack
smack	smirk	plunder	wail	hew
strike	snigger	pilfer	weep	slit

hair-raising	big-headed	crazy	garrulous
have kittens	blow one's own trumpet	have a screw loose	have the gift of the gab
petrified	conceited	off one's head	hold one's tongue
fly off the handle	slip one's mind	get the sack	hard up
hit the roof	have a memory like a sieve	on the dole	in the red
irate	amnesia	made redundant	make ends meet

CARD 1A

Ask: *What's the word for...*

1 a way of pronouncing a language, particular to one area? (7)

2 a general pardon, especially of prisoners? (4)

3 the crime of deliberately setting fire to property? (6)

4 food used to attract fish or animals so that they can be caught? (1)

5 a building where soldiers live? (3)

6 the crime of demanding money from someone in return for keeping something secret? (8)

7 the group of actors performing a play? (2)

8 the workers on a ship? (5)

Answer: *It's definition number (1).
         It's...(read out the definition)*

FOLD

CARD 1B

Say: *Give a definition of the word:*

1 bait (4)

2 cast (7)

3 barrack (5)

4 amnesty (2)

5 crew (8)

6 arson (3)

7 accent (1)

8 blackmail (6)

Answer: *It's word number (1).
         It's...(read out the noun)*

CARD 2A

Ask: *What's the word for...*

1 a violent storm with strong winds? (7)

2 a narrow channel for water? (5)

3 a heavy shower of rain? (1)

4 a disease which a large number of people have at the same time? (4)

5 a time when there is very little food in an area and the people go hungry? (8)

6 money paid by or to a bank on a loan? (2)

7 rubbish thrown away in a public place? (6)

8 the brutal killing of large numbers of people? (3)

Answer: *It's definition number (1).
         It's...(read out the definition)*

FOLD

CARD 2B

Say: *Give a definition of the word:*

1 downpour (3)

2 interest (6)

3 massacre (8)

4 epidemic (4)

5 ditch (2)

6 litter (7)

7 cyclone (1)

8 famine (5)

Answer: *It's word number (1).
         It's...(read out the noun)*

CARD 3A

Ask: *What's the word for...*

1 a person, usually a woman, who helps at the birth of a child? (3)

2 an announcement, usually in a newspaper, of a person's death, with information about his or her life? (7)

3 the child or children of two people? (4)

4 a person whose parents are dead? (8)

5 a piece of clothing worn over others to keep them clean? (1)

6 a single sheet of glass in a window? (5)

7 a piece of land almost completely surrounded by water? (2)

8 a small hole in the ground full of water? (5)

Answer: *It's definition number (1).*
It's...(read out the definition)

FOLD

CARD 3B

Say: *Give a definition of the word:*

1 overalls (5)

2 peninsula (7)

3 matron (1)

4 offspring (3)

5 pane (6)

6 puddle (8)

7 obituary (2)

8 orphan (4)

Answer: *It's word number (1).*
It's...(read out the noun)

CARD 4A

Ask: *What's the word for...*

1 money paid to kidnappers to make them release a prisoner? (7)

2 a person escaping from danger and seeking shelter? (3)

3 a cure for a disease? (1)

4 a noisy and violent disturbance by a crowd? (8)

5 a safe place for people, or for birds and animals? (6)

6 a bag, often on a frame, used for carrying things on your back? (4)

7 the skin on your head? (2)

8 the front of the leg between the knee and the ankle? (3)

Answer: *It's definition number (1).*
It's...(read out the definition)

FOLD

CARD 4B

Say: *Give a definition of the word:*

1 remedy (3)

2 scalp (7)

3 refugee (2)

4 rucksack (6)

5 shin (8)

6 sanctuary (5)

7 ransom (1)

8 riot (4)

Answer: *It's word number (1).*
It's...(read out the noun)

CARD 5A	CARD 5B
Ask: *What's the word for...*	Say: *Give a definition of the word:*
1 a high-pitched scream? (2)	1 sleet (4)
2 a large metal container for rubbish? (5)	2 shriek (1)
3 a window in the roof of a building? (8)	3 slogan (5)
4 a mixture of rain and snow? (1)	4 stench (7)
5 a catchy phrase used in advertising? (3)	5 skip (2)
6 a husband or wife? (6)	6 spouse (6)
7 an unpleasant smell? (4)	7 tantrum (8)
8 a sudden fit of bad temper? (7)	8 skylight (3)
Answer: *It's definition number (1).* *It's...(read out the definition)*	Answer: *It's word number (1).* *It's...(read out the noun)*

FOLD

48 DEFINITIONS CARDS 2: VERBS

CARD 1A	CARD 1B
Ask: *Which verb means...*	Say: *Give a definition of the verb:*
1 to run away suddenly and hide because you have done something wrong or against the law? (4)	1 to drag (8)
2 to walk at an easy, gentle rate? (3)	2 to char (4)
3 to shout loudly and angrily? (7)	3 to amble (2)
4 to cause something to become black by burning? (2)	4 to abscond (1)
5 to hold closely? (6)	5 to dash (7)
6 to have a strong, almost uncontrollable desire for something? (8)	6 to clasp (5)
7 to run a short distance suddenly and quickly? (5)	7 to bellow (3)
8 to pull without lifting, especially along the ground? (1)	8 to crave (6)
Answer: *It's definition number (1).* *It's...(read out the definition)*	Answer: *It's word number (1).* *It's...(read out the verb)*

FOLD

CARD 2A	CARD 2B
Ask: *Which verb means…*	Say: *Give a definition of the verb:*

CARD 2A

Ask: *Which verb means…*

1 to wait in hiding for someone and to attack them by surprise? (3)

2 to murder a ruler, politician, etc. for political reasons or reward? (8)

3 to listen secretly to a private conversation? (1)

4 to steal for your own use money that is placed in your care? (5)

5 to kill off all the creatures or people in a place? (2)

6 to burn unsteadily? (7)

7 to look steadily at something? (4)

8 to hear a private conversation by accident? (6)

Answer: *It's definition number (1).*
    It's…(read out the definition)

FOLD

CARD 2B

Say: *Give a definition of the verb:*

1 to eavesdrop (3)

2 to exterminate (5)

3 to ambush (1)

4 to gaze (7)

5 to embezzle (4)

6 to overhear (8)

7 to flicker (6)

8 to assassinate (2)

Answer: *It's word number (1).*
    It's…(read out the verb)

CARD 3A

Ask: *Which verb means…*

1 to have a quick incomplete view of something? (2)

2 to sleep through the winter? (4)

3 to walk in an awkward way, or with difficulty? (7)

4 to steal in small amounts? (1)

5 to examine closely? (8)

6 to look fiercely and angrily at something? (3)

7 to wait about, not wanting to leave? (6)

8 to think something over carefully? (5)

Answer: *It's definition number (1).*
    It's…(read out the definition)

FOLD

CARD 3B

Say: *Give a definition of the verb:*

1 to pilfer (4)

2 to glimpse (1)

3 to glare (6)

4 to hibernate (2)

5 to ponder (8)

6 to linger (7)

7 to hobble (3)

8 to scrutinize (5)

Answer: *It's word number (1).*
    It's…(read out the verb)

CARD 4A	**CARD 4B**

Ask: *Which verb means...*

Say: *Give a definition of the verb:*

CARD 4A	CARD 4B
1 to shout angrily and wildly as if mad? (2)	1 to scamper (3)
2 to burn skin and flesh by contact with hot liquid or vapour? (5)	2 to rave (1)
3 to run quickly with short steps? (1)	3 to trudge (8)
4 to walk very unsteadily? (8)	4 to recite (6)
5 to shine strongly and brilliantly? (6)	5 to scald (2)
6 to repeat aloud, usually from memory? (4)	6 to blaze (5)
7 to shine brightly in small flashes, for example, a diamond? (7)	7 to glitter (7)
8 to walk slowly and with effort? (3)	8 to stagger (4)

Answer: *It's definition number (1).*
       It's...(read out the definition)

Answer: *It's word number (1).*
       It's...(read out the verb)

FOLD

CARD 5A	**CARD 5B**

Ask: *Which verb means...*

Say: *Give a definition of the verb:*

CARD 5A	CARD 5B
1 to fall like a waterfall? (1)	1 to cascade (1)
2 to burn to ashes (usually a dead body)? (5)	2 to execute (4)
3 to sleep lightly? (7)	3 to hurl (8)
4 to kill as a punishment, usually after a trial? (2)	4 to glow (7)
5 to throw wildly, without careful aim? (6)	5 to cremate (2)
6 to take a quick look at something? (8)	6 to fling (5)
7 to give out heat and/or light without flames or smoke? (4)	7 to doze (3)
8 to throw very strongly? (3)	8 to glance (6)

Answer: *It's definition number (1).*
       It's...(read out the definition)

Answer: *It's word number (1).*
       It's...(read out the verb)

FOLD

49 OPPOSITES CARDS

CARD 1A	**CARD 1B**
Ask: *What's number (1)?*	Ask: *What's number (1)?*
1 blunt (s____)	1 sharp (b____)
2 mean (g____)	2 generous (m____)
3 cowardly (b____)	3 brave (c____)
4 stale (f____)	4 fresh (s____)
5 bright (d____)	5 dim (b____)
6 generous (m____)	6 mean (g____)
Answer: *It's... (give the opposite of the word)*	Answer: *It's... (give the opposite of the word)*

FOLD

CARD 2A	**CARD 2B**
Ask: *What's number (1)?*	Ask: *What's number (1)?*
1 tiny (e____)	1 enormous (t____)
2 careful (c____)	2 careless (c____)
3 accidental (d____)	3 deliberate (a____)
4 voluntary (c____)	4 compulsory (v____)
5 deep (s____)	5 shallow (d____)
6 foreign (n____)	6 native (f____)
Answer: *It's... (give the opposite of the word)*	Answer: *It's... (give the opposite of the word)*

FOLD

CARD 3A

Ask: *What's number (1)?*

1 conceal (r____)
2 attack (d____)
3 reject (a____)
4 deny (a____)
5 succeed (f____)
6 divide (u____)

Answer: *It's… (give the opposite of the word)*

CARD 3B

Ask: *What's number (1)?*

1 reveal (c____)
2 defend (a____)
3 accept (r____)
4 admit (d____)
5 fail (s____)
6 unite (d____)

Answer: *It's… (give the opposite of the word)*

CARD 4A

Ask: *What's number (1)?*

1 noisy (q____)
2 cheerful (m____)
3 odd (number) (e____)
4 rough (s____)
5 absent (p____)
6 simple (c____)

Answer: *It's… (give the opposite of the word)*

CARD 4B

Ask: *What's number (1)?*

1 quiet (n____)
2 miserable (c____)
3 even (number) (o____)
4 smooth (r____)
5 present (a____)
6 complicated (s____)

Answer: *It's… (give the opposite of the word)*

CARD 5A

Ask: *What's number (1)?*

1 joy (m____)
2 success (f____)
3 wealth (p____)
4 victory (d____)
5 profit (l____)
6 reward (p____)

Answer: *It's… (give the opposite of the word)*

CARD 5B

Ask: *What's number (1)?*

1 misery (j____)
2 failure (s____)
3 poverty (w____)
4 defeat (v____)
5 loss (p____)
6 punishment (r____)

Answer: *It's… (give the opposite of the word)*

FOLD

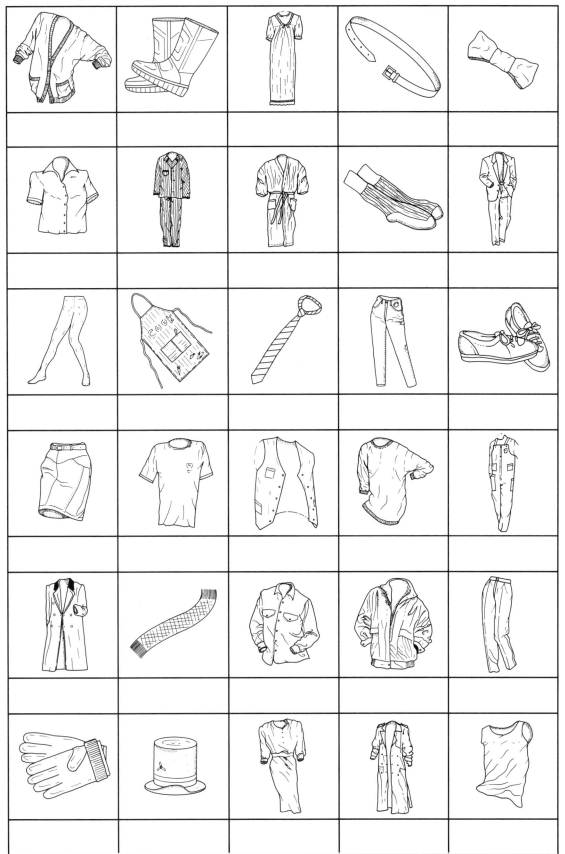

1	apron	gloves	2	belt	tie	3	blouse	suit
	cardigan	pyjamas		scarf	vest		hat	tights
	jacket			skirt			jumper	

4	boots	socks	5	dress	T-shirt	6	bow tie	shirt
	coat	shoes		jeans	trousers		dressing gown	waistcoat
	overalls			nightdress			raincoat	

51 BOARD GAME 2: SYNONYMS

adore	amaze	ascend	assist	ban
bicker	build	cease	cheat	clutch
consider	dawdle	detest	display	flog
flourish	force	forecast	gleam	join
jump	mock	plunder	quiver	reply
rotate	scare	scurry	shout	start

1	aid	quarrel	**2**	astound	revolve	**3**	climb	predict
	end	thrash		forbid	swindle		contemplate	yell
	leap			loot			idolize	
4	commence	respond	**5**	connect	loiter	**6**	construct	shake
	exhibit	scamper		frighten	ridicule		glisten	
	loathe			grasp	compel		prosper	

52   BOARD GAME 3: FOUR OF A KIND

aluminium copper tin	beech oak willow	bin urn vase	ant earwig cockroach	collar lining pocket
cod salmon sole	barge steamer yacht	tramp vagabond wanderer	eye level radar	stage stalls wings
bungalow cottage shack	blackbird eagle owl	alligator snake tortoise	flock herd pack	ferret fox wolf
barley oats wheat	arson fraud murder	buttercup carnation cowslip	banana peach plum	hoe shears rake
basil parsley thyme	ham lamb venison	ladle mincer saucepan	boot tyre windscreen	crab lobster prawn
plane pliers screwdriver	asparagus leek onion	audience onlookers spectators	juvenile teenager youth	avalanche drought earthquake

1		2		3	
gnat lizard trunk	veal zinc	badger congregation haddock	tangerine yew	adolescent famine grater	madam turnip

4		5		6	
chisel mansion mint	shoal vagrant	circle crayfish magpie	perjury wheelbarrow	clutch hem poppy	rye trawler

53 BOARD GAME 4: THREE-IN-A-ROW (Board)

1	2	3	4	5
◯	◯	◯	◯	◯
6	7	8	9	10
◯	◯	◯	◯	◯
11	12	13	14	15
◯	◯	◯	◯	◯
16	17	18	19	20
◯	◯	◯	◯	◯
21	22	23	24	25
◯	◯	◯	◯	◯
26	27	28	29	30
◯	◯	◯	◯	◯

53 BOARD GAME 4: THREE-IN-A-ROW (Questions)

Square 1

- What's the opposite of *compulsory*? (*voluntary*)
- Her hair is usually blonde. But she went to the hairdresser's last week and now it's black. What has she done to her hair? (*She has dyed it.*)
- What's the missing preposition in this sentence: She is very good _____ tennis. (*at*)
- Where would you expect to find a pillow? (*On a bed.*)
- What is a hand part of? a clock / a car / a typewriter (*a clock*)
- Is this right or wrong? This is Mr Brown. He's a widow. His wife died last Christmas. (*Wrong. It should be widower.*)

Square 2

- Which of these is correct: It's hot. Let's sit in the shade. / It's hot. Let's sit in the shadow. (*shade*)
- What is the opposite of *brave*? (*cowardly*)
- What is a young cat called? (*a kitten*)
- The room at the bottom of a house is called the cellar. What's the room at the top of a house called? (*the attic*)
- What's the English word for a bad dream? (*a nightmare*)
- It's quite unbelievable. What's a synonym for *unbelievable*? (*incredible*)

Square 3

- Which word does not go with the others: petal / trunk / stem / daffodil (*Trunk – all the others are to do with a flower.*)
- Is this right or wrong? The word *parting* has something to do with hair. (*Right. It's the line dividing the hair.*)
- The river is deep here. What's the opposite of *deep*? (*shallow*)
- What sort of table would you usually have in the living room – perhaps in front of the sofa? (*a coffee table*)
- Which of these is correct: Can you remember me to post the letter? / Can you remind me to post the letter? (*remind*)
- What's the piece of glass in a window called? (*a pane*)

Square 4

- Her hair wasn't real. She was wearing a _____. What? (*wig*)
- It's my birthday today. What would you say to me in English instead of *Happy Birthday!* (*Many happy returns (of the day)!*)
- Which animal bleats? a frog / a pig / a lamb (*a lamb*)
- You come to see me if you want to buy or sell a house. What's my job? (*an estate agent*)

- What word in English do we use to describe such things as ghosts, flying saucers, telepathy and so on – things that can't be explained naturally? (*the supernatural*)
- What do you say in Britain if someone sneezes? (*Bless you!*)

Square 5

- What is the opposite of *innocent*? (*guilty*)
- Which of the following is correct: I feel pity for her. / I feel sorry for her. (*I feel sorry for her.*)
- If you are feeling *dead beat* you are: hungry / very tired / ill (*very tired*)
- I won't be long. I'm just going to the launderette. What do you think I'm going to do? (*Wash clothes. / Do the washing.*)
- Which of the following is correct? Take your seats please, the play is about to start. / Take your places please, the play is about to start. (*seats*)
- What is the opposite of *satisfied*? (*dissatisfied*)

Square 6

- Is this right or wrong? (At the theatre) There will be a fifteen-minute pause between Acts one and two. (*Wrong. It should be fifteen-minute interval.*)
- This is my brother's son. He's my _____. What? (*nephew*)
- Is this right or wrong? The person in charge of an orchestra is called the director. (*Wrong. He is called the conductor.*)
- Which of these is correct? The nature in Switzerland is beautiful. / The landscapes in Switzerland is beautiful. / The scenery in Switzerland is beautiful. (*scenery*)
- If you felt peckish what would you feel like doing? (*Eating something. It means you are slightly hungry.*)
- What is the missing preposition in this sentence: You must put more effort _____ your work. (*into*)

Square 7

- Can you walk very far if you are unconscious? (*No. You can't walk at all.*)
- What is the opposite of *temporary*? (*permanent*)
- What sound does a cat make when it's happy? (*It purrs.*)
- What's a synonym for *very, very tired*? It starts with the letter *e*. (*exhausted*)
- To help you to understand a foreign programme on television, you often have words underneath the picture. What are these words called? (*sub-titles*)
- What do mothers put their babies in when they take them out for walks? (*prams/pushchairs*)

Square 8

- Which of these means *He let me sleep at his place for the night*?
  He put me up. / He put me away. / He put me in. (*He put me up.*)
- What is the person in charge of the day-to-day running of a newspaper called? (*the editor*)
- What do you think of when you hear the following words?
  surgeon / matron / ward / theatre (*a hospital*)
- Which of the following is *not* an animal?
  squirrel / hedgehog / cowslip / tortoise (*Cowslip – it's a flower; the others are animals.*)
- Is this right or wrong?
  Lying in the sun can often make you feel rather drowsy. (*Right. It means it can make you feel sleepy.*)
- This bread is fresh. What's the opposite of *fresh*? (*stale*)

Square 9

- Which of the following words is the odd man out?
  circulation / leader / column / channel (*Channel – all the others are to do with a newspaper.*)
- What's the missing preposition in this sentence:
  Don't forget – you must be home _____ 10.30 at the latest. (*by*)
- In Britain would you wear a vest over or under your shirt? (*under*)
- What do we call a person who lives in one town but travels to another town to work? (*a commuter*)
- Which of the following words is a synonym for *obstinate*?
  mean / stubborn / affectionate (*stubborn*)
- He owed the bank £5,000. He was £5,000 in _____. What? (*debt*)

Square 10

- How might you feel if you looked down from the top of a very high building? (*giddy/dizzy*)
- What do we call the doctor who performs operations at a hospital? (*a surgeon*)

- Is this right or wrong?
  "I'm afraid it's very serious, Mrs Brown. Your husband's got heartburn." (*wrong*)
- What's the missing preposition in this sentence?
  He went abroad _____ business. (*on*)
- What do you think of when you hear the words *bark, trunk, willow* and *branch*? (*a tree*)
- Which of these is correct?
  He checked my passport. / He controlled my passport. (*checked*)

Square 11

- Which of the following is a synonym for *hate*?
  desist / loathe / disgust (*loathe*)
- Which of these is correct?
  I must bathe the baby. / I must bath the baby. (*bath*)
- How many eyes do you close when you wink? (*one*)
- If you want to stop your trousers from falling down, you can wear a belt or a pair of _____. What? (*braces*)
- Which of the following do we get from a sheep?
  lamb / veal / beef / ham (*lamb*)
- It doesn't fit me. This means:
  It's the wrong colour. / It's the wrong style. / It's the wrong size. (*It's the wrong size.*)

Square 12

- In the fifties women wore stockings. But now they mostly wear _____ instead. What? (*tights*)
- What sound does a dog make? (*It barks. / It growls.*)
- I'm suffering from *insomnia*. What can't I do? (*sleep/go to sleep*)
- Is this right or wrong?
  A female sheep is called a ewe. (*right*)
- Which of the following means *they quarrelled*?
  They fell apart, / They fell through. / They fell out. (*They fell out.*)
- What's the opposite of *sharp*? (*blunt*)

Square 13

- What can you take with you on holiday (apart from a dictionary) to help you to ask for something in a foreign language? (*a phrase book*)
- Which word in English do we use to describe a person who can speak two languages fluently? (*bilingual*)
- What's the opposite of *voluntary*? (*compulsory*)
- My sister and I were born on the same day. We are _____. What? (*twins*)
- You are not allowed to pick this flower by law. It's _____. What? (*protected*)
- Where would you find a lapel? (*On a jacket.*)

Square 14

- "I'm a great tennis player. I'm really brilliant! I've won every match. No one can beat me! I'm the greatest!"
  What is this person doing? (*boasting / bragging*)
- To walk under a ladder means that you will have bad luck. What do we call a belief like this? (*a superstition*)
- What is a core part of?
  a flower / a bicycle / an apple (*An apple – the inside.*)
- What word beginning with *e* do we use to describe a man who behaves in a very feminine way. We say he is _____. What? (*effeminate*)
- This is my uncle's son. He is my _____. What? (*cousin*)
- This disease can be passed on by touch. What word do we use to describe this? This disease is _____. What? (*contagious*)

Square 15

- What do people have on their roofs to enable them to watch television? (*an aerial / a satellite dish*)
- What is the name given to a long journey by boat? (*a voyage*)
- What is the missing preposition in this sentence?
  We went to Australia _____ sea. (*by*)
- What do we call a person who breaks into houses or buildings in order to steal from them? (*a burglar*)
- If you are broke, this means that you don't have any _____. What? (*money*)
- What is the yellow part of an egg called? (*the yolk*)

Square 16

- Where would you wear a beret? (*On your head.*)
- My wife is in hospital expecting a baby. Where in the hospital is she? (*In the maternity ward.*)
- Which of these is correct?
  Yesterday I bought a new pillow for the sofa. / Yesterday I bought a new cushion for the sofa. (*cushion*)
- What is the opposite of *vanish*? (*appear*)
- If you can make up your own stories to tell to your children at bedtime then you must be quite _____. What? (*imaginative*)
- What would you use in Britain to dry the dishes? (*a tea towel*)

Square 17

- Which of these is correct?
  Is there space in the car for me as well? / Is there room in the car for me as well? (*room*)
- What do we call someone who can't read or write? (*illiterate*)

- What disease is this?
  His neck and mouth are swollen. He's got _____. What? (*mumps*)
- What is this person's job?
  He or she checks where cars are parked. He or she is a _____. What? (*traffic warden*)
- What do we call the alphabetical list at the back of books, where names, subjects and so on are given, plus the page on which they can be found? (*an index*)
- What do we call the person who calls out the score in a tennis match? (*the umpire*)

Square 18

- You don't usually say a *slice* of bacon in Britain. What do you say instead? (*rasher*)
- Which of the following is not an insect:
  beetle / badger / ant / ladybird (*badger*)
- Which animal neighs? (*a horse*)
- What is the list of things to be discussed at a meeting called? (*the agenda*)
- Which verb means to stay away from school without permission? (*to play truant*)
- Where would you find portholes? (*On a ship. They're the round windows.*)

Square 19

- What is the missing preposition in the following sentence?
  He died _____ cancer at the age of seventy-three. (*of*)
- Which word means to run away secretly in order to get married – usually without the permission of one's parents? (*to elope*)
- Is this right or wrong?
  The person in charge of a museum is called the curate. (*Wrong. He or she is a curator. A curate is a type of priest.*)
- What could you say instead of *the dog attacked him*?
  The dog went away with him. / The dog went in for him. / The dog went for him. (*The dog went for him.*)
- Is your instep part of your hand / arm / foot? (*Foot – it's the middle part of the foot from the toes to the ankle.*)
- The words *pram*, *cot* and *nappy* all have something to do with _____. What? (*a baby / babies*)

Square 20

- What is a rung part of? (*A ladder – you put your foot on it.*)
- What is a trigger part of? (*A gun – you pull it to fire the gun.*)
- Which of the following people would use an easel?
  an artist / a photographer / an electrician
  (*an artist*)
- What do British people call the Friday before Easter? (*Good Friday*)
- What do British people call December 26th? (*Boxing Day*)
- Which word beginning with *e* means to listen secretly to a private conversation? (*to eavesdrop*)

Square 21

- What is the missing preposition in the following sentence?
  He hates losing _____ cards. (*at*)
- What does the expression *to thumb a lift* mean? (*to hitchhike*)
- The words *bark, lead* and *kennel* all have something to do with _____. What? (*a dog / dogs*)
- Which speaker might be slightly frightened?
  I was startled. / I was amazed. / I was astounded. (*startled*)
- A person who is very tall and thin is called which of these words:
  skinny / lanky / stocky? (*lanky*)
- The words *clubs, spades* and *deal* all have something to do with _____. What? (*cards / playing cards*)

Square 22

- Which of the following people would use a baton?
  a policeman / a conductor / an undertaker
  (*A conductor – he holds it in his hand.*)
- If a friend says he can *put you up* this means he can:
  give you a lift home / offer you somewhere to sleep / lend you a ladder? (*offer you somewhere to sleep*)
- What do you call a house where all the rooms are on one floor? (*a bungalow*)
- Complete the following:
  A _____ of bees. (*swarm*)
- Dawn is the time of day when light first appears. What do we call the time of day when daylight is fading? (*dusk / twilight*)
- Which word beginning with *a* means to murder a ruler or a politician for political reasons or reward? (*to assassinate*)

Square 23

- Which of the following is not part of a car?
  a boot / a bonnet / a deck / a clutch (*a deck*)
- What is the word for the line of holes made in paper to help you to tear it?
  punctures / staples / perforations (*perforations*)
- The water is very deep here. What's the opposite of deep? (*shallow*)
- Which of the following is an example of crockery?
  a cup / a banana / a knife / a nephew (*a cup*)
- All these words mean *to pull*, but which do we use when one car is pulling another?
  to haul / to tug / to tow (*to tow*)
- Two people of completely opposite character are as different as:
  bread and cheese / water and cheese / chalk and cheese (*chalk and cheese*)

Square 24

- Which of these is a place where a river meets the sea?
  a gulf / a bay / an estuary / an inlet (*an estuary*)
- All these are sounds we make when we are amused. Which is the loudest?
  a giggle / a chuckle / a guffaw (*a guffaw*)
- Finish this proverb. As old as _____.
  Samson / the hills / dry bread (*the hills*)
- Which of these is not a hat?
  a bowler / a cravat / a beret (*a cravat*)
- Which of these is nearest in meaning to *to put up with*?
  to tolerate / to permit / to allow (*to tolerate*)
- The parts of a wheel which join the middle to the outside edge are the _____. What?
  rays / spokes / bars (*spokes*)

Square 25

- Which man is tired?
  He strode along the street. / He trudged along the street. / He wandered along the street.
  (*He trudged along the street.*)
- All these verbs mean *to damage* in one way or another. Which one means with a weapon?
  to discolour / to slit / to corrode (*To slit – to cut, usually with a knife.*)
- I got the sack last week. This means I _____. What?
  had a baby / lost my job / was in bed ill
  (*lost my job*)
- Which of these is not part of your clothing?
  a hem / a sleeve / a hat trick (*A hat trick – it's when the a player scores three goals in a football match.*)
- Your nearest relative is your _____. What?
  closest kin / first kin / next of kin (*next of kin*)
- Finish this phrase:
  As right as _____.
  fog / sleet / rain (*rain*)

Square 26

- Complete this phrase:
  As cool as _____.
  an iceberg / ice-cream / a cucumber
  (*a cucumber*)
- Finish this sentence:
  Don't beat about the _____.
  tree / bush / garden path (*bush*)
- In Britain where might you see the sign
  'To let'?
  outside a house / on a car / inside a hotel
  (*Outside a house – it means you can rent it.*)
- Finish this proverb:
  One man's meat is another man's _____.
  poison / drink / fish (*poison*)
- An American says *period* when a British person
  says _____. What?
  comma / colon / full stop (*full stop*)
- When you promise not to talk about something,
  you say _____. What?
  I won't whisper a word. / I won't breathe a
  word. / I won't tell a word. (*I won't breathe a
  word.*)

Square 27

- An American says *streetcar* when a British
  person says _____. What?
  tram / family car / coach (*tram*)
- Finish this proverb:
  Two's company, three's _____.
  a mob / a crowd / a congregation (*a crowd*)
- Something that is done secretly or slyly is
  _____. What?
  offhand / underhand / hand in glove
  (*underhand*)
- To stop someone talking, you would _____.
  What?
  gag him / handcuff him / bind him (*gag him*)
- Which word would you *not* use to describe
  flowers?
  a bunch / a bouquet / a cluster (*a cluster*)
- Finish this proverb:
  A bird in the hand is worth two in the _____.
  tree / bush / forest (*bush*)

Square 28

- An American says *freeway* when a British
  person says _____. What?
  main road / dual carriageway / motorway
  (*motorway*)
- Finish this proverb:
  _____ is the mother of invention.
  Luck / Want / Necessity (*Necessity*)
- Is a magpie a fish or a bird? (*a bird*)
- If I am *well-off* I am _____. What? (*rich*)
- What would you be doing if you were having
  forty winks?
  swimming / sleeping / eating (*sleeping*)
- Give a synonym for *stubborn*. (*obstinate* /
  pig-headed)

Square 29

- An American talks about *a janitor* when a
  British person says _____. What?
  a cleaner / a porter / a caretaker (*a caretaker*)
- Who would you expect to use handcuffs?
  (*a policeman*)
- Complete the following:
  A _____ of stairs. (*flight*)
- Is a budgie a popular pet in Britain? (*Yes. It's a
  small bird, some of which can be trained to talk.*)
- What do we call a child who hits smaller or
  weaker children? (*a bully*)
- If you suffer from dyslexia, you have difficulty in
  _____. What?
  walking / reading / sleeping (*reading*)

Square 30

- Is the following true or false?
  I hate the flat I'm living in at present. I'm really
  homesick! (*False. Homesick means that you are
  unhappy when away from home.*)
- If you were suspicious, you might say *I smell a
  _____*. What?
  cat / horse / rat (*rat*)
- Could you climb ladders if you suffered from
  vertigo? (*No. It's a fear of heights.*)
- An unmarried man is called a bachelor. What's
  an unmarried woman called? (*a spinster*)
- Is a cockroach an insect or a bird? (*an insect*)
- Give another word for *drawback*. (*disadvantage*)

an umbrella	niece	a rabbit	blonde
borrow	a foreigner	birthday	spell
floor	the capital	beard	ring
department store	on holiday	neighbour	at the weekend
cheap	move	camera	the ironing
a book	mother	a bike	striped
join	a stranger	wedding	work
room	the centre	eye	watch
shoe shop	at work	customer	last week
expensive	visit	lake	the stairs

54 COMPLETE THE SENTENCES (Teacher's sheet)

Read out the following sentences in this order.

1 It's raining. You'd better take _____ with you. (*an umbrella*)

2 My sister has two children, a boy and a girl. My nephew is called Paul and my _____ Sarah. (*niece*)

3 I love animals. I've got three pets – a cat, a dog and _____. (*a rabbit*)

4 She was a beautiful and famous model, with blue eyes and long, _____ hair. (*blonde*)

5 I don't buy many books. I usually _____ them from the library instead. (*borrow*)

6 He isn't from this country. He's _____. (*a foreigner*)

7 It's David's _____ on Saturday. He's 17. Are you going to his party? (*birthday*)

8 "How do you _____ rubber?"
   "R-U-double B-E-R." (*spell*)

9 He lives in a small flat on the second _____. (*floor*)

10 Copenhagen is _____ of Denmark. (*the capital*)

11 He was a tall man with curly hair and a thick, black _____. (*beard*)

12 Peter and I have just got engaged. Would you like to see my _____? (*ring*)

13 Harrods is a large and very famous _____ in London. (*department store*)

14 Mr Brown isn't here this week, I'm afraid. He's _____ in Spain. (*on holiday*)

15 Let me introduce you to my _____, Jackie Smith. She and I have lived next door to each other for nearly eight years. (*neighbour*)

16 Shall we got to Brighton _____? We can leave after work on Friday. (*at the weekend*)

17 This dress was really _____. It only cost me ten pounds. (*cheap*)

18 My husband and I are tired of living in Britain. We've decided to _____ to Canada. (*move*)

19 Smile everyone and look at the _____! (*camera*)

20 I hate doing housework – especially _____. (*the ironing*)

wished	round	journey	exactly
disappointed	wife	return	rain
lightning	knocking	standing	dripped
clothes	without	off	other
breakfast	spend	afraid	blue
happily	sensitive	certain	unless
waited	through	exhibition	therefore
excited	neighbour	travel	snow
lighter	shouting	sitting	rushed
shoes	after	among	next
dinner	keep	sorry	white
slowly	sensible	obvious	although

Read out the following story, leaving gaps.

The Princess and the Pea

by Hans Christian Andersen

Once upon a time there was a prince who (*wished*) to marry a princess. Only it had to be a real princess. He travelled all (*round*) the world to find one and, during his (*journey*), he found many. But there was always something wrong. He could not say (*exactly*) what it was, but first one thing, then another didn't seem quite right. In the end, feeling tired and (*disappointed*), he returned to his palace, unhappy that he had not found a real princess to be his (*wife*).

One evening, shortly after his (*return*), there was a terrible storm. The (*rain*) poured down and there were flashes of (*lightning*) and loud roars of thunder.

Suddenly, there was a loud (*knocking*) on the palace door and the old king, the prince's father, went to open it. Who should be (*standing*) there but a beautiful princess, or so she claimed. But she looked terrible! Her hair hung limp and wet, drops of water (*dripped*) from her nose, and her (*clothes*) clung like rags to her body. But she said she was a real princess.

The king took her to see the queen.
"We'll soon see about that!!" muttered the old queen to herself. (*Without*) saying a word, she went quietly to the spare bedroom. There, she took all the bedclothes (*off*) the bed, and put a little pea on the bottom of it. Then she laid twenty mattresses one upon the (*other*) on top of the little pea. Next she put twenty eiderdowns upon the mattresses. This was the bed the princess was to sleep in.

Next morning, when the lovely princess came down to (*breakfast*), the king, queen and prince looked at her closely, for the queen had told the others what she had done.
"Excuse me, my dear," said the old queen. "How did you (*spend*) the night? I hope you slept well."
The princess looked at her with tired eyes and said with a sigh, "Oh dear! I'm (*afraid*) not! I had an awful night. I hardly slept at all! Goodness knows what was in my bed, but it felt so hard and lumpy underneath me. I'm black and (*blue*) all over!"

The king, queen and prince started smiling (*happily*). It was plain that the lady was a real princess. For she had felt the little pea through twenty mattresses and twenty eiderdowns. No one but a true princess could have such (*sensitive*) skin.

The prince was delighted and married her because at last he was (*certain*) that he had found a real princess. As for the little pea, it was put on a marble stand and exhibited in the Royal Museum. It is still there to this day, (*unless*) of course, it has been lost.

(Adapted from *Fairy Tales retold by James Riordan*, © 1987 Octopus Books Ltd, p. 107)

56 TYPES OF PEOPLE

Listen to your teacher reading out 16 definitions, and then write down what you think the correct word is. Choose from the following:

accomplice	castaway	hooligan	picket
adjudicator	conscript	invigilator	sibling
arbitrator	expatriate	midwife	spouse
beneficiary	hermit	patriot	teetotaller

1 _____

2 _____

3 _____

4 _____

5 _____

6 _____

7 _____

8 _____

9 _____

10 _____

11 _____

12 _____

13 _____

14 _____

15 _____

16 _____

56 TYPES OF PEOPLE (Teacher's sheet)

Read out the sentences in this order. Say the number before reading out the sentence.

1 This is someone who supervises people taking an examination. He or she makes sure they don't cheat. (*invigilator*)

2 This is a single word for husband or wife. (*spouse*)

3 This is someone who has deliberately withdrawn from society and lives completely alone. (*hermit*)

4 This is someone who helps another person commit a crime. (*accomplice*)

5 This is someone who, during a strike, is placed outside a factory by his or her trade union to try to prevent other workers from going in until the strike is over. (*picket*)

6 This is someone who is called in to settle a dispute between two people or groups – usually at the request of both sides (e.g. during a strike). (*arbitrator*)

7 This is someone who has been shipwrecked. (*castaway*)

8 This is someone who loves his or her country and feels very loyal towards it. (*patriot*)

9 This is someone who is appointed to act as a judge in a competition. (*adjudicator*)

10 This is someone who never drinks alcohol. (*teetotaller*)

11 This is someone who is made to serve in a country's army, navy or air force whether he or she wants to or not. (*conscript*)

12 This is a person who is entitled to receive money or property from a will or insurance policy. (*beneficiary*)

13 This is someone who is living in a foreign country. (*expatriate*)

14 This is a noisy, rough person (usually young), who causes damage or disturbance in public places. (*hooligan*)

15 This is a nurse who has been specially trained to advise pregnant women and to assist them when giving birth. (*midwife*)

16 This is a single word for brother or sister. (*sibling*)

57 MISSING WORDS: NOUNS

Choose the correct noun to complete each of the following sentences.

1 Britain has a professional army, so _____ is no longer needed.

2 You told me you paid £2,000 for your computer, yet the bill comes to £1,250. How do you explain the _____?

3 *To pass away* is a(n) _____ for *to die*.

4 "Don't put all your eggs in one basket" is an old _____.

5 "Swinging London" was in its _____ in the 1960s.

6 As far as I know, there is no known _____ for this poison.

7 Before getting the part in the new musical she had to attend a(n) _____.

8 A(n) _____ was held to determine the wishes of the people regarding nuclear power.

9 No one doubts nowadays that there is a strong _____ between smoking and lung cancer.

10 According to the _____ on the wall, Richard Burton was born here.

11 After the divorce, Mrs Piper was awarded _____ of the children.

12 As it was her first offence, the magistrate showed _____ and let her off with a warning.

13 When I returned from my holiday, there was a(n) _____ of work waiting for me.

14 I don't really have time to read the report now, Claire. Could you give me the _____ of it?

15 My uncle always reads the _____ column in *The Times* every morning just to make sure he is still alive.

16 His grandmother died, leaving him a small _____.

conscription	discrepancy
euphemism	proverb
heyday	antidote
audition	referendum
correlation	plaque
custody	clemency
backlog	gist
obituary	legacy

58 WORDS OF SIMILAR MEANING: ADJECTIVES

Add a word which is similar in meaning to each group.

1 colossal, enormous, huge _____

2 calm, peaceful, still _____

3 dirty, foul, unclean _____

4 brave, gallant, heroic _____

5 artful, crafty, deceitful _____

6 fierce, savage, vicious _____

7 dangerous, unsafe, risky _____

8 obstinate, stubborn, headstrong _____

9 exhausted, fatigued, tired _____

10 humble, meek, modest _____

11 frightful, hideous, ugly _____

12 depressed, sad, unhappy _____

13 courteous, friendly, polite _____

14 aggressive, hostile, militant _____

15 complex, complicated, involved _____

16 hasty, impulsive, rash _____

immense	tranquil
polluted	courageous
sly	ferocious
perilous	wilful
weary	lowly
repulsive	dejected
civil	belligerent
intricate	impetuous

59 MATCHING PAIRS: (ADJECTIVE + NOUN)

Complete the following phrases with a suitable noun.

1 a juicy _____

2 a roaring _____

3 a cool _____

4 a comfortable _____

5 a helpless _____

6 a narrow _____

7 a loyal _____

8 an even _____

9 a piercing _____

10 a fragrant _____

11 a delicious _____

12 a haunted _____

13 an ingenious _____

14 a tricky _____

15 an infectious _____

16 an urgent _____

17 a cotton _____

18 a shallow _____

19 a poisonous _____

20 a steep _____

orange	fire	breeze	chair
invalid	escape	friend	number
scream	smell	meal	house
plan	problem	disease	message
dress	pool	snake	hill
statue	calendar	reputation	occasion
estimate			

60 WHAT DOES IT MEAN? 1

Listen and write the numbers 1–16 next to the correct sentences.

a "I'm at the end of my tether!" _____

b "I'm at a loose end." _____

c "My hair stood on end!" _____

d "You could have knocked me down with a feather!" _____

e "My lips are sealed." _____

f "I'm in a rut." _____

g "I lost my head." _____

h "I blew my top." _____

i "I've got the gift of the gab." _____

j "I've got green fingers." _____

k "I was tickled pink!" _____

l "I had a lump in my throat." _____

m "He led me up the garden path." _____

n "I got hot under the collar." _____

o "It slipped my mind." _____

p "I was given the sack." _____

60 WHAT DOES IT MEAN? 1 (Teacher's sheet)

Read out the sentences in this order:

1 Write the number 1 next to the person who has promised to keep a secret. (*e   My lips are sealed.*)

2 Write the number 2 next to the person who forgot to do something. (*o   It slipped my mind.*)

3 Write the number 3 next to the person who was very sad and was about to start crying. (*l   I had a lump in my throat.*)

4 Write the number 4 next to the person who has no patience or strength left. (*a   I'm at the end of my tether.*)

5 Write the number 5 next to the person who is good at gardening. (*j   I've got green fingers.*)

6 Write the number 6 next to the person who was terrified. (*c   My hair stood on end!*)

7 Write the number 7 next to the person who became angry and excited. (*n   I got hot under the collar.*)

8 Write the number 8 next to the person who doesn't have anything to do. (*b   I'm at a loose end.*)

9 Write the number 9 next to the person who lost his or her job. (*p   I was given the sack.*)

10 Write the number 10 next to the person who is leading a boring way of life which is difficult to change. (*f   I'm in a rut.*)

11 Write the number 11 next to the person who was very surprised. (*d   You could have knocked me down with a feather!*)

12 Write the number 12 next to the person who panicked. (*g   I lost my head.*)

13 Write the number 13 next to the person who was very amused at something. (*k   I was tickled pink!*)

14 Write the number 14 next to the person who is good at talking. (*i   I've got the gift of the gab.*)

15 Write the number 15 next to the person who lost his or her temper. (*h   I blew my top.*)

16 Write the number 16 next to the person who was misled or deceived. (*m   He led me up the garden path.*)

61 WHAT DOES IT MEAN? 2

Listen and write the numbers 1–16 next to the correct sentences.

a "I've been taken for a ride." _____

b "I've just had forty winks." _____

c "I must tighten my belt." _____

d "I've let the cat out of the bag." _____

e "I've put my foot in it." _____

f "I've turned over a new leaf." _____

g "I'm in two minds about it." _____

h "They fell off the back of a lorry!" _____

i "I've been cooking the books." _____

j "I've got butterflies in my stomach." _____

k "I'm on my last legs." _____

l "I'm over the moon." _____

m "There are no flies on me!" _____

n "I'm a bit thin on top." _____

o "I smell a rat." _____

p "I've lost my tongue." _____

61 WHAT DOES IT MEAN? 2 (Teacher's sheet)

Read out the sentences in this order:

1 Write the number 1 next to the person who is speechless.
(*p I've lost my tongue.*)

2 Write the number 2 next to the person who is extremely happy and excited. (*l I'm over the moon.*)

3 Write the number 3 next to the person who has reformed, has become a better person. (*f I've turned over a new leaf.*)

4 Write the number 4 next to the person who has some things he or she has stolen. (*h They fell off the back of a lorry!*)

5 Write the number 5 next to the person who doesn't have much hair or is becoming bald. (*n I'm a bit thin on top.*)

6 Write the number 6 next to the person who has altered the accounts of a company in order to deceive. (*i I've been cooking the books.*)

7 Write the number 7 next to the person who has revealed a secret, probably accidentally. (*d I've let the cat out of the bag.*)

8 Write the number 8 next to the person who would be difficult to deceive. (*m There are no flies on me!*)

9 Write the number 9 next to the person who is going to economize. (*c I must tighten my belt.*)

10 Write the number 10 next to the person who is undecided about something. (*g I'm in two minds about it.*)

11 Write the number 11 next to the person who has had a short sleep. (*b I've just had forty winks.*)

12 Write the number 12 next to the person who has made an embarrassing mistake. (*e I've put my foot in it.*)

13 Write the number 13 next to the person who is suspicious about something. (*o I smell a rat.*)

14 Write the number 14 next to the person who is close to death. (*k I'm on my last legs.*)

15 Write the number 15 next to the person who has been deceived or tricked by someone. (*a I've been taken for a ride.*)

16 Write the number 16 next to the person who is feeling nervous. (*j I've got butterflies in my stomach.*)

gaze	glance	glare	peer	stare
dash	limp	stagger	stroll	trudge
can't stand	despise	detest	hate	loathe
eavesdrop	lisp	mumble	overhear	stutter
frown	grin	leer	pout	scowl
bark	bleat	bray	neigh	purr

63 THE HOMOPHONE GAME (Teacher's sheet)

Read out the words one at a time. Allow the students approximately 30–40 seconds to write down two possible words.

List 1

1 meet / meat
2 our / hour
3 steal / steel
4 hear / here
5 stair / stare
6 dear / deer
7 their / there
8 sum / some
9 flower / flour
10 right / write
11 tale / tail
12 weather / whether
13 pair / pear
14 here / hear
15 wear / where
16 red / read
17 son / sun
18 week / weak
19 way / weigh
20 eight / ate

List 2 (more difficult)

1 place / plaice
2 boulder / bolder
3 maze / maize
4 scent / cent
5 waste / waist
6 mail / male
7 lesson / lessen
8 bear / bare
9 piece / peace
10 sell / cell
11 sail / sale
12 mist / missed
13 him / hymn
14 board / bored
15 hair / hare
16 rain / reign
17 sight / site
18 feet / feat
19 tears / tiers
20 course / coarse

divorce (n)	complain (vb)
emigrate (vb)	hitchhike (vb)
biography (n)	lonely (adj)
cheerful (adj)	pregnant (adj)
brochure (n)	slippery (adj)
choir (n)	arrest (vb)
exaggerate (vb)	witness (n)
crawl (vb)	disobedient (adj)
boring (adj)	profit (n)
voluntary (adj)	dictator (n)

swede	mumps
freckles	headline
core	beak
twig	relay
umpire	yolk
knuckle	cuff
cot	canvas
keyboard	petal
lobe	hand
earwig	gear lever

vegetable	disease
face	newspaper
apple	bird
tree	athletics
tennis	egg
hand	shirt
baby	painting
computer	flower
ear	clock
insect	car

CARD 1: DESCRIBING PERSONALITY

Write your answers on a separate piece of paper.

1 He's marvellous at making up stories to tell his children at bedtime. He's so i_____.

2 My daughter wants to be a success and get on in life. She's very a_____.

3 My brother is cheerful one minute and miserable the next. He's so m_____.

4 Most girls and boys of 16 or 17 are far too i_____ to get married and have children.

5 David doesn't like his wife dancing with other men. He gets very j_____.

6 My husband and I love meeting people and going to parties. We're very s_____.

7 He has a very high opinion of himself. He's very b_____-h_____.

8 John's so p_____. I don't think he's ever been late for work or a meeting in his life.

9 I hate having to wait for anything. I'm terribly i_____.

10 She never gets annoyed or upset if anything goes wrong. She's a very e_____-g_____ person.

CARD 2: CARS AND MOTORING

Write your answers on a separate piece of paper.

1 The three pedals on the floor of a car are called (from left to right) the c_____, the b_____ and the a_____.

2 After starting your car, don't forget to release the h_____ before you drive away.

3 To o_____ another car means to drive past it.

4 If you pass a driving test you are issued with a d_____ l_____.

5 Most motorways are divided into three l_____. The inside one is for the slowest vehicles.

6 In Britain there is a 30 m.p.h. s_____ l_____ in built-up areas.

7 For safety reasons you should always wear a s_____.

8 There are s_____ s_____ along most motorways where you can stop to buy petrol, have a meal, etc.

9 You keep your luggage in the b_____ of a car.

10 A b_____ is a main road which takes traffic around a town rather than through its centre.

CARD 3: HOUSE AND HOME

Write your answers on a separate piece of paper.

1 Some people paint the walls of their living rooms. Others prefer to use w_____.

2 Most modern houses have c_____ h_____ instead of open fires.

3 A room under a house where you can live is called a b_____.

4 If you want to save time when cooking, then you should buy a m_____ o_____.

5 The postman delivers letters through the l_____.

6 Smoke comes out of a c_____.

7 We don't have curtains in the bedroom, we have b_____ instead.

8 My sister doesn't live in a house, she lives in a very modern b_____ of f_____.

9 Doors made of glass which open out into the garden are called F_____ w_____.

10 In Britain the money you borrow to buy a house is usually referred to as a m_____.

CARD 4: BOOKS, etc.

Write your answers on a separate piece of paper.

1 A c_____is a book or booklet which gives you a list of goods for sale plus their prices.

2 You keep a personal record of events in a d_____.

3 The n_____ *War And Peace* was written by Leo Tolstoy.

4 When something goes wrong with your car, you can always try to repair it with the help of the car m_____.

5 If you're not sure where to go on holiday, why don't you get a holiday b_____ from your nearest travel agent?

6 If you don't know a person's telephone number, you can always look it up in the telephone d_____.

7 If you want to know what a word means, look it up in a d_____.

8 You can use a p_____ b_____ to help make yourself understood when visiting a foreign country.

9 An e_____ is a book or group of books dealing with every branch of knowledge in alphabetical order.

10 *Vogue* is one of the most famous fashion m_____ in the world.

CARD 5: EDUCATION

Write your answers on a separate piece of paper.

1 Music, English and Mathematics are different sorts of s_____.

2 The s_____ are the teachers working in a school.

3 In Britain, you must go to school between the ages of five and sixteen. It's c_____.

4 The person in charge of a school is called the h_____.

5 You have to pass your exams at school to go on to u_____. The most famous ones in Britain are Oxford and Cambridge.

6 In Britain the school year is divided into three t_____.

7 If you want to know at what time your lesson is, look at the t_____.

8 A b_____school is a school where pupils live. They only go home to their families during the holidays.

9 The school British children go to when they are five is called a p_____ school.

10 Then at the age of eleven or twelve they go on to a s_____ school.

1	2	3	4
5	6	7	8
9	10	11	12
13	14	15	16
17	18	19	20

1 apple banana pear	**2** dog horse lion	**3** bookcase chair table	**4** bathroom kitchen living room
5 cabbage carrot onion	**6** cup mug plate	**7** butcher pilot teacher	**8** golf rugby tennis
9 bicycle car van	**10** London Rome Stockholm	**11** rain sunshine wind	**12** brother mother sister
13 green orange violet	**14** orange juice tea water	**15** ant fly spider	**16** spring summer winter
17 scarf shirt tie	**18** guitar piano violin	**19** hotel library shop	**20** American Dutch Turkish

1 beside besides	**2** foreigner stranger	**3** quite quiet	**4** meeting reunion
5 lose loose	**6** employer employee	**7** remember remind	**8** fun funny
9 discover invent	**10** their there	**11** bath bathe	**12** lucky happy
13 alone lonely	**14** sensible sensitive	**15** driver chauffeur	**16** blink wink
17 lend borrow	**18** teacher professor	**19** pass an exam take an exam	**20** recipe receipt

70   20-SQUARE 3: SYNONYMS

1 huge (e--r---s)	2 mad (i---n-)	3 disappear (v----h)	4 frightened (s--r-d)
5 rich (w--lt--)	6 obstinate (s--b---n)	7 brag (b---t)	8 awful (d---d---)
9 strange (p-c--i--)	10 impolite (r--e)	11 allow (p--m--)	12 dizzy (g---y)
13 keen (e---r)	14 wonderful (m---el---s)	15 alter (c--n--)	16 dependable (r-l--b--)
17 evil (w--k--)	18 annoyed (i---t---d)	19 choose (s---c-)	20 hard-working (i-d--t----s)

71 20-SQUARE 4: EXPLAIN THE WORDS

1 a *huge* garden	**2** a *previous* tenant	**3** a *priceless* painting	**4** a *disused* mine
5 a black *beetle*	**6** a *scarlet* blouse	**7** an *illiterate* man	**8** to *limp* along the street
9 an *affectionate* person	**10** a pleasant *chat*	**11** to *loathe* housework	**12** to work *conscientiously*
13 a *temporary* job	**14** a *convicted* criminal	**15** a £10,000 *ransom*	**16** a £40,000 *mortgage*
17 a *plump* woman	**18** the *average* salary	**19** a *courteous* child	**20** to *call off* a meeting

1 **st-**	2 **-le**	3 **-ic**	4 **sh-**
5 **pr-**	6 **re-**	7 **-se**	8 **fl-**
9 **sc-**	10 **in-**	11 **-ful**	12 **de-**
13 **-ing**	14 **tr-**	15 **-an**	16 **-ive**
17 **-ous**	18 **-ed**	19 **dis-**	20 **-ent**

1 DEFENDANT'S SPEECH ENDS IN LONG SENTENCE	**2** POLICE DISCOVERED SAFE UNDER A BLANKET	**3** GIRL HAD A DETECTIVE IN HER BOOT	**4** PLEASE HELP OUR NURSES HOME!
5 POLICE SHOOT MAN WITH KNIFE	**6** POLITICIANS TO DISCUSS RUBBISH	**7** LUNG CANCER IN WOMEN MUSHROOMS	**8** TRAFFIC DEAD RISE SLOWLY
9 DRUNK GETS NINE MONTHS IN VIOLIN CASE	**10** LOST: BLACK CAT, MALE. REWARD (ONE BLACK EYE)	**11** PRESIDENT WINS ON BUDGET, BUT MORE LIES AHEAD	**12** POLICE WITH TRACKER DOGS FAIL TO FIND LEAD
13 PASSENGERS HIT BY CANCELLED TRAINS	**14** MPS TO ACT TO KEEP THEATRES OPEN	**15** MINERS REFUSE TO WORK AFTER DEATH	**16** CRASH COURSES FOR PRIVATE PILOTS
17 MICHAEL JACKSON APPEALS TO POPE	**18** ANGRY BULL INJURES FARMER WITH A GUN	**19** STOLEN PAINTING FOUND BY TREE	**20** FOUR-POSTER BED. 102 YEARS OLD. PERFECT FOR ANTIQUE LOVER.

74 20-SQUARE 7: EXPLAIN THE IDIOM

1 a storm in a teacup	**2** to hit the roof	**3** to get cold feet	**4** to turn a blind eye to something
5 at the eleventh hour	**6** to catch someone red-handed	**7** to let the cat out of the bag	**8** to pull the wool over someone's eyes
9 to be at a loose end	**10** to smell a rat	**11** to keep a straight face	**12** to talk shop
13 to beat about the bush	**14** to cook the books	**15** to pay through the nose for something	**16** to be a wet blanket
17 to be all fingers and thumbs	**18** to put one's foot in it	**19** to pull someone's leg	**20** to be off-colour

75 THE ALPHABET RACE

See how quickly you can work out the following.

A B C D E F G H I J K L M N O P Q R S T U V W X Y Z

1 What's the 14th letter of the alphabet? _____

2 What's the 7th letter from the end of the alphabet? _____

3 Make two words starting with the 4th letter of the alphabet. _____

  _____

4 Make a word from the 1st, 20th, 7th and 15th letters of
  the alphabet. _____

5 How many different letters appear in the word
  embarrassed? _____

6 Make two words that end in the 20th letter of the alphabet. _____

  _____

7 Which letters in the word *society* come between D and P
  in the alphabet? _____

8 Which letter in the word *skirt* is furthest from N in the
  alphabet? _____

9 Which letter occurs twice in *realise* and once in *scream*? _____

10 Which letters occur most often in *interesting*? _____

11 What is the position in the alphabet of the middle letter
   in the word *advertisement*? _____

12 Which letter is halfway between the 5th and 15th letters
   of the alphabet? _____

13 Arrange the following words in alphabetical order:

   crab   comb   carrot   cream   cotton _____

   _____

   _____

   _____

   _____

14 Which letter in the word *hair* is closest to *n* in the
   alphabet? _____

15 Make a word that includes the 1st and 16th letters of the
   alphabet. _____

76 WORD HUNT

Name at least two things that:

1 are very expensive. _____

2 you can use to write with. _____

3 have a nice smell. _____

4 are small enough to fit in your pocket. _____

5 are dangerous. _____

6 can make you feel happy. _____

7 are thin and sharp. _____

8 you can wear above the waist. _____

9 you would find it difficult to live without. _____

10 are yellow. _____

11 make an unpleasant or loud noise. _____

12 are very heavy. _____

13 you shouldn't eat if you are on a diet. _____

14 people enjoy doing in their free time. _____

15 are found in the country (but not usually in a town). _____

16 can move very quickly. _____

17 won't work without electricity. _____

18 you usually only use once. _____

19 are found in a kitchen. _____

20 people usually take with them on holiday. _____

21 are containers. _____

22 you can do to stop a baby crying. _____

23 are very fragile. _____

24 can make you feel tired. _____

25 people are usually frightened of. _____

26 are made of glass. _____

27 taste nice. _____

28 men find attractive about women, or vice versa. _____

29 cost less than a pound. _____

30 you can do to stop a nosebleed. _____

77 NEW WORDS FROM OLD

Which noun can you add to all four words to form new single-word nouns or two-word nouns?
(Note: the noun can be added before or after the word.)

Example: hand**bag**, kit**bag**, **bag**pipes, sleeping **bag**

1   band, chair, fire, pit   _____

2   end, guide, mark, scrap   _____

3   board, Christmas, credit, score   _____

4   hanger, over, rain, waist   _____

5   back, dark, shoe, rocking   _____

6   candle, flood, house, sky   _____

7   clip, news, wall, weight   _____

8   battle, friend, space, wreck   _____

9   fall, proof, salt, melon   _____

10 basket, eye, snow, room   _____

11 bath, service, class, changing   _____

12 arm, woman, push, wheel   _____

13 guest, hold, boarding, wife   _____

14 box, card, goal, lamp   _____

15 bathe, light, set, burn   _____

16 room, cup, dash, key   _____

17 ache, land, letter, strong   _____

18 head, coast, dead, up   _____

19 cloth, coffee, spoon, time   _____

20 page, cow, friend, hood   _____

21 chair, hole, kind, snow   _____

22 father, foot, ladder, in   _____

23 chatter, gear, room, post   _____

24 flower, coffee, hole, tea   _____

25 cut, horse, line, net   _____

78 PUZZLE IT OUT

There are five people staying at a hotel: Mr Petty, Mr Grove, Mrs Williams, Ms Stevens and Mr Harvey. Use the clues to complete the chart with the information below.

Room number	101	102	103	104	105
Name					
Job					
Character					
Interest/hobby					
Other information					

Job	Character	Interest/hobby
solicitor	sociable	painting
estate agent	conceited	bird-watching
surgeon	bossy	amateur dramatics
traffic warden	mean	tennis
plumber	optimistic	gardening

Other information

is a widower
is Australian
is a twin
is bald
is bilingual

Ms Stevens usually looks on the bright side of life.

The man in room 101 loves going to parties and meeting people.

The person who works at a hospital is from down-under.

Mr Grove doesn't like telling strangers what his job is – especially not motorists.

Mr Harvey sold two houses last week.
The person in the room next to him often deals with divorces and wills.

The person who wears a uniform to work has green fingers.

The woman who speaks German as well as she speaks English hates spending money.

The tradesman has a dress rehearsal tonight.

The person who loves ordering people about has an end room.

Mr Harvey has been an ornithologist for nearly twenty years.

The estate agent's wife passed away last year.

Mrs Williams has an excellent serve.

The person with a tanned scalp has a very high opinion of himself.

The person in the room next to the plumber often visits Art galleries.

Mr Petty is in the room between Ms Stevens and Mrs Williams.

The traffic warden's brother was born half an hour before him.

The optimist is staying in room 102.

The solicitor hopes to play at Wimbledon one day.

The person in room 104 never tips.

Mr Harvey is in room 105.

79 FIND THE WORDS

Read through the newspaper articles below and see if you can work out what the missing words are. There are twelve different words altogether, numbered 1–12.

THE GANG WITH THE WORST SENSE OF DIRECTION

A team of criminals planned a raid on a Peterborough newsagent's _____(1)_____ down to the last detail. In the middle of the _____(2)_____ they knocked a hole _____(3)_____ an outside wall, carefully removing one brick at a _____(4)_____ until they could climb into the room where the safe was kept.

They worked for several _____(5)_____ until at last they broke _____(3)_____. However, they _____(6)_____ themselves standing, not in the strong room, but a lavatory which was locked _____(7)_____ the other side. They collected up their tools and went _____(8)_____ empty-handed.

THE GREATEST CRIMINAL COINCIDENCE

In the early _____(5)_____ of Sunday morning, two raiders bent over a safe in a grocer's _____(1)_____ in Fulham High Street. They heard a noise and were gathering up their tools and preparing to run _____(9)_____ two figures appeared in the doorway.

They were two more burglars arriving to rob the safe at exactly the _____(10)_____ _____(4)_____. The four of them introduced themselves and _____(11)_____ to join forces to carry the half-ton safe out of the building.

They were trying to open it with an acetylene torch at a garage _____(9)_____ the _____(12)_____ arrived and arrested them. _____(9)_____ they opened the safe they _____(6)_____ more than £100 inside.

THE WORST ATTEMPT TO REPEAT A CRIMINAL SUCCESS

A thief _____(7)_____ Kansas City threw a brick _____(3)_____ a plate glass window of a jewellery _____(1)_____, filled his bag and disappeared into the _____(2)_____.

Back _____(8)_____, he thought about how easy it had been and _____(11)_____ to go back again. A few days later, using the _____(10)_____ technique, he pulled off another smash-and-grab at the _____(10)_____ store. It was the start of several identical raids until the management, tired of replacing the window, fitted an armour plate one.

Unaware of this, the thief arrived once again at the _____(1)_____, carrying a large brick under his arm. Unfortunately, _____(9)_____ he threw it at the window, it bounced straight back, struck him on the head and knocked him out. He was still unconscious _____(9)_____ the _____(12)_____ arrested him.

(From *Criminal Records* by Graham Nown, Futura Publications 1987, pp. 52, 56, 61.)

Word 1 _____	Word 5 _____	Word 9 _____
Word 2 _____	Word 6 _____	Word 10 _____
Word 3 _____	Word 7 _____	Word 11 _____
Word 4 _____	Word 8 _____	Word 12 _____

80 TRUE OR FALSE 1

You must bet between 10 and 100 points for each statement.

Statement	True	False	Bet	Loss	Gain
1 It's raining. You'd better take an **umbrella** with you.	❏	❏	_____	_____	_____
2 I don't have any money – I'm **bald**.	❏	❏	_____	_____	_____
3 I couldn't eat any more, thank you. I'm **fed up**.	❏	❏	_____	_____	_____
4 I need a **saucepan** to boil these potatoes.	❏	❏	_____	_____	_____
5 The customs officer **controlled** our passports.	❏	❏	_____	_____	_____
6 He was born in Berlin. He's **Dutch**.	❏	❏	_____	_____	_____
7 You usually wear a **belt** around your waist.	❏	❏	_____	_____	_____
8 "Have a nice weekend." "Thank you. **Same again, please**."	❏	❏	_____	_____	_____
9 When you buy something, you are usually given a **recipe**.	❏	❏	_____	_____	_____
10 I'm **starving**. I'd better put a warm coat on.	❏	❏	_____	_____	_____
11 My cousin buys and sells houses. She's an **estate agent**.	❏	❏	_____	_____	_____
12 This is my **niece**, Doreen. She's my brother's wife.	❏	❏	_____	_____	_____
13 He's very **generous**. He's always buying me presents.	❏	❏	_____	_____	_____
14 I love meeting people. I'm very **sociable**.	❏	❏	_____	_____	_____
15 You usually find a **grater** in the living room.	❏	❏	_____	_____	_____

Total losses/gains: _____ _____

GRAND TOTAL:
(Gains minus losses)

81 TRUE OR FALSE 2

You must bet between 10 and 100 points for each statement.

Statement	True	False	Bet	Loss	Gain
1 You wouldn't say very much if you were **unconscious**.	❏	❏	_____	_____	_____
2 Most people would like to be a **hostage** if they were given the chance.	❏	❏	_____	_____	_____
3 Most gardeners are proud of their **weeds**.	❏	❏	_____	_____	_____
4 A **rung** is part of a ladder.	❏	❏	_____	_____	_____
5 You usually keep a **dustbin** in the kitchen.	❏	❏	_____	_____	_____
6 **Surgeons** spend a lot of time in the theatre.	❏	❏	_____	_____	_____
7 We can't eat this bread – it's **mouldy**.	❏	❏	_____	_____	_____
8 I'm very **supernatural**. I never walk under ladders, for example.	❏	❏	_____	_____	_____
9 **Capital punishment** used to be very common in British schools.	❏	❏	_____	_____	_____
10 In Britain you usually wear a **vest** under your shirt.	❏	❏	_____	_____	_____
11 It's very hot. Let's sit in the **shadow**.	❏	❏	_____	_____	_____
12 He must have run all the way – he's **panting**.	❏	❏	_____	_____	_____
13 **Sub-titles** are connected with a newspaper.	❏	❏	_____	_____	_____
14 A **petal** is part of a bicycle.	❏	❏	_____	_____	_____
15 **Long Johns** are worn by men.	❏	❏	_____	_____	_____

Total losses/gains: _____ _____

GRAND TOTAL: ⟨ ⟩
(Gains minus losses)

82 TRUE OR FALSE 3

You must bet between 10 and 100 points for each statement.

Statement	True	False	Bet	Loss	Gain
1 He acts in a very feminine way; he's very **ephemeral**.	❑	❑	_____	_____	_____
2 If a person is **coy**, he or she is rather shy and bashful.	❑	❑	_____	_____	_____
3 To **bicker** means to quarrel.	❑	❑	_____	_____	_____
4 Most monks live in an **abattoir**.	❑	❑	_____	_____	_____
5 A **dulcet** sound is very unpleasant to the ear.	❑	❑	_____	_____	_____
6 A **polyglot** is very good at languages.	❑	❑	_____	_____	_____
7 There's no one living in this building – it's **derelict**.	❑	❑	_____	_____	_____
8 He kept his school books in a **hammock** on his back.	❑	❑	_____	_____	_____
9 A **hod** is used by a bricklayer.	❑	❑	_____	_____	_____
10 Most actors would be thrilled if a critic described their performance as **soporific**.	❑	❑	_____	_____	_____
11 The words *deal*, *suit* and *clubs* all have something to do with **playing cards**.	❑	❑	_____	_____	_____
12 A **rostrum** has something to do with gardening.	❑	❑	_____	_____	_____
13 A **trilby** is something you wear.	❑	❑	_____	_____	_____
14 A female sheep is called a **ewe**.	❑	❑	_____	_____	_____
15 **Urbane** means to do with towns or cities.	❑	❑	_____	_____	_____

Total losses/gains: _____ _____

GRAND TOTAL:
(Gains minus losses)

blou	se	cret
rea	ch	oir
toa	st	ream
op	en	emy
eag	le	ather
came	ra	zor
cl	ap	ple
spo	on	ion
bo	at	tack
cent	re	ason
pil	ot	her
cab	in	vent
cem	ent	rance
yell	ow	ner
wom	an	swer
pret	ty	pical

84 ARRANGE THE WORDS

Here is an alphabetical list of 50 words to describe people. Place each word under one of the headings below.

absent-minded, active, affectionate, ambitious, arrogant, assertive, boastful, brave, cautious, charitable, cheeky, cheerful, compassionate, conscientious, considerate, cowardly, cunning, decent, envious, frivolous, generous, hard-working, haughty, humble, impulsive, irresponsible, jealous, just, mean, naive, obedient, obstinate, optimistic, patient, pessimistic, possessive, pretentious, proud, reserved, rude, ruthless, self-confident, selfish, sensitive, sociable, tactless, talkative, tolerant, vain, witty

Good qualities		Faults		Both/Can't decide

85 IT'S QUIZ TIME: IDIOMS

Read through the following questions and write your answers on a separate piece of paper.

1 What kind of party is a **stag party**?

2 If you were at a restaurant and the person with you offered to **go Dutch**, what would this mean?

3 Our postman **kicked the bucket** last week. What has happened to him?

4 A tiresome, irritating person is often described as **a pain** in what part of the body?

5 Jim's **behind bars**. Where is he?

6 Amanda's **down in the mouth** today. How is she feeling?

7 Why wouldn't you normally go to a party in your **birthday suit**?

8 What sort of a relationship would you have with someone if you **got on like a house on fire**?

9 Why are **blacklegs** generally unpopular?

10 My uncle has been given a **golden handshake.** What has happened to him?

11 Where on the body would you find **crow's feet**?

12 How would you be behaving towards someone if you were **giving him or her the cold shoulder**?

13 What does a **gate-crasher** usually do?

14 How would you be feeling if you were **full of beans**?

15 Where (or what) would you be if you were **in the land of Nod**?

16 What's a **busman's holiday**?

17 What are you doing when you **name the day**?

18 What sort of person is an **early bird**?

19 Why don't people usually like **playing gooseberry**?

20 I've just bought **the local rag**. What have I bought?

86 VERB + NOUN COLLOCATIONS

Complete the table below by adding two more words or phrases for each verb. Choose from the following. (You can use each word or phrase once only.)

a cold, a conclusion, a law, a living, advantage of someone, attention, a speech, a tooth, a trap for someone, between the lines, corners, fire, gear, interest in something, music, offence, one's leg, one's mind, one's temper, permission, sentence (*at court*), someone a compliment, thanks, the curtains, the fort, the ice, the impression, the line, the table, the way

ASK	a question		
BREAK	a promise		
CATCH	a bus		
CHANGE	money		
CUT	one's finger		
DRAW	a picture		
GIVE	advice		
HOLD	a meeting		
LAY	eggs		
LOSE	one's job		
MAKE	a profit		
PASS	the butter		
PAY	a bill		
READ	a book		
TAKE	a seat		

87 SORT OUT THE TEXT 1

In the following text there are letters missing from various words. See how well you can read the text, adding the missing letters.

The parrot and the conjuror

Have you heard about the conjuror who used to entertain the passengers every night on board ship?

Well, ev--- night h- gave h-- show, a-- every ti-- he d--, a par--- used to s-- not f-- away, wi-- his bea-- eyes fix-- on h--.

And wh-- the conj---- hid a ca-- up h-- sleeve, t-- parrot wo--- croak: "It's u- his sle---!" And wh-- he slip--- a rab--- in his poc---, the par--- would cr---: "Down his trou----, down his trou----!"

The conj---- was dy--- to wring his ne--.

But o-- night, wh-- the conj---- was i- the mid--- of his tri---, the sh-- hit an iceb---, broke in t--, and sa-- almost immed------. The conj---- found him---- in the wa--- and thrashed ab--- to ke-- afloat, until he event----- managed to pu-- himself u- on to an em--- raft. He flopped on-- it, absol----- exhausted. A-- who sho--- be perched on t-- far si-- of the ra-- too? The par---. And the par---'s beady ey-- were fi--- on the conj----.

The conj---- just l-- there, flat o--, for nea--- an ho--. And a-- the while the par--- never stir---, and he nev-- for one sec--- took h-- eyes o-- the conj----.

Finally, t-- conjuror mo---, and ope--- his ey--. And the par--- croaked: "All ri---, I gi-- up. Where's the ship?"

(Extract from *The Puffin Joke Book* by Bronnie Cunningham, 1974. First published in Puffin Books, 1974)

88 SORT OUT THE TEXT 2

The following newspaper article is completely mixed up. See if you can put it in the right order by numbering the lines 1–27. (Some numbers have already been filled in.)

Lucky Chris falls from 22 floors up then walks away

12	A stunned passer-by rushed to give him the kiss of life, but
	absolute miracle he survived. He must have fallen more than
	'comfortable'. He has a broken elbow, neck injuries and minor
	down and walked away. Security guards watching on a video
1	A man plunged 200 ft from the top of a tower block yesterday –
	hospital.
	but there wasn't a spot of blood anywhere."
	of scrap.
	They could not believe their eyes when Chris, 26, climbed
	roof of a parked car.
	John Whalley, caretaker at the flats said yesterday: "It's an
	and walked away almost unhurt. Chris Saggers sailed past
	200 ft and he must have been going at a fair old speed. There
	student, was planning to sell it. Now he's the owner of a pile
	from the flattened Nissan Micra car and headed off up a
	Police later found him wandering nearby and took him to
	twenty two floors of a block of flats before landing on the
	The owner of the eight-year-old car, a Salford University
	cuts and bruises.
	Seconds later, he climbed out of the wreckage, dusted himself
	a very-much-alive Chris muttered: "I'm fine" and walked off.
21	Chris, who lives near Salford, was taken to nearby Hope
	monitor at the council flats in Salford, Greater Manchester,
	Hospital where his condition last night was described as
	were convinced he was falling to certain death.
	was glass everywhere and the car was a complete write-off,
	side street.

(From the *Daily Express*, Saturday April 3 1993)

89 SORT OUT THE PUNCH LINES

In the following 12 jokes, the punch lines have got mixed up. See if you can work out which punch line belongs to which joke.

Joke 1

Man If you really are a police officer, then why on earth are you wearing that red and yellow patterned suit?

Policeman Oh dear! What shape should it be, then?

Joke 2

Ironmonger Can I help you, sir?

Customer I'd like a mousetrap, please. And hurry – I've got a bus to catch.

Ironmonger It's too late now – it's flown away!

Joke 3

Boy I say, what a lovely coloured cow over there!

Girl It's a Jersey.

Boy Don't be stupid! That's the new rabbit hutch!

Joke 4

Customer I'll have four nice lamb chops, please. And make them lean.

Butcher All right. Here's a paper bag.

Joke 5

Mechanic The trouble with your car is simple, sir. The battery's flat.

Man Oh, I didn't know it was electric.

Joke 6

Woman My budgie lays square eggs.

Man That's amazing! Can it talk as well?

Woman Yes, but only one word.

Man What's that?

Woman Sorry, sir – we don't make them that big.

Joke 7

Teacher Did you miss school yesterday, Jane?

Jane Just a routine check, sir.

Joke 8

Patient Doctor, my hair's falling out. I want something to keep it in.

Doctor Certainly, sir. Which way?

Joke 9

It was the Royal Wedding.

Father Where's your mum?

Daughter She's upstairs waving her hair.

Father Ouch!

Joke 10

Neighbour How's your wife?

Man Oh, she's ill. She's very, very ill.

Neighbour Oh, I'm sorry to hear that. Is that her coughing?

Man No sir, not a bit.

Joke 11

Salesman Right, here's your new bath, madam. Do you want a plug for it?

Woman Can't we afford a flag?

Joke 12

Boy Dad! Dad! I've been stung by a wasp.

Dad Don't worry, son. I'll put some special cream on it.

Boy Really? I thought it was its skin.

90 WHO WROTE WHAT?

Try to work out who wrote the books below. Choose from the following authors.

Peter Out	Ellen Back	Neil Downe	C. Ment
Sue Nora Later	Trudy Light	Anne Teak	Teresa Green
Miss D. Buss	Constance Norah	Laura Norder	Liza Lott
Willie Maykit	Lord Howard Hertz	B. Keeper	San Widge
Lee King	Claude Legg	U.R.A. Payne	Walter Wall

A Hole In My Bucket by _____

A Visit To The Dentist by _____

Bricklaying by _____

Carpet Fitting For All by _____

Crime Does Not Pay by _____

Fade Away by _____

How To Tame Lions by _____

In The Country by _____

A Long Walk by _____

Making Snack Meals by _____

My Happiest Days by _____

Not Quite The Truth by _____

Parachute Jumping by _____

Sleepless Nights by _____

The Sunday Service by _____

It Was Bound To Happen by _____

The Naughty Boy by _____

The Worst Journey In The World by _____

Very Old Furniture by _____

How To Make Honey by _____